Praise for *Understanding Jim Crow* and the ~~Jim C.~~

"One of the most important contributions to the study of American history that I have ever experienced."
—Henry Louis Gates Jr., director of the W.E.B. Du Bois Institute for African American Research

"For decades the author has been on a Pilgrimage to bring out from our dank closets the racial skeletons of our past. His is a crucial mission, because he forces us to realize that race relations grew *worse* in the first several decades of the twentieth century— something many Americans never knew or now want to suppress. This book allows us to see, even *feel* the racism of just a generation or two ago—and Pilgrim shows that elements of it continue, even today. See it! Read it! Feel it! Then help us all transcend it!"
—James W. Loewen, author of *Lies My Teacher Told Me* and coeditor of *The Confederate and Neo-Confederate Reader*

"This was a horrific time in our history, but it needs to be taught and seen and heard. This is very well done, very well done."
—Malaak Shabazz, daughter of Malcolm X and Betty Shabazz

"The museum's contents are only a small part of the damaging effects of the Jim Crow laws that were found all across America, including bright and sunny California. This history is not only an important part of understanding where America was but, in an age of states making it harder and harder for citizens to vote, it is relevant to note that we have been here before."
—Henry Rollins, host of the History Channel's *10 Things You Don't Know About*

"The museum has been one of my treasured go-to resources for teaching people about the deep-seated roots of the racism that persists in our collective subconscious. Only by facing our history and its hold on our psyche can we construct a better culture. This work is invaluable."
—damali ayo, author of *How to Rent a Negro* and *Obamistan! Land without Racism*

Understanding Jim Crow

Using Racist Memorabilia to Teach Tolerance
and Promote Social Justice

David Pilgrim

BTL

Understanding Jim Crow: Using Racist Memorabilia to Teach Tolerance and Promote Social Justice
David Pilgrim
Copyright © 2015 Ferris State University and PM Press
All rights reserved. No part of this book may be transmitted by any means without permission in writing from the publisher.

ISBN: 978-1-62963-114-1

Library of Congress Control Number: 2015930901

Cover by John Yates/Stealworks
Interior design by briandesign

10 9 8 7 6 5 4 3 2 1

PM Press
PO Box 23912
Oakland, CA 94623
www.pmpress.org

This edition first published in Canada in 2015 by Between the Lines
401 Richmond Street West, Studio 277, Toronto, Ontario, M5V 3A8, Canada
1–800–718–7201
www.btlbooks.com

Canadian cataloguing information is available from Library and Archives Canada.

ISBN 978-1-77113-250-3   Between the Lines paperback
ISBN 978-1-77113-251-0   Between the Lines epub
ISBN 978-1-77113-252-7   Between the Lines pdf

Printed in the USA by the Employee Owners of Thomson-Shore in Dexter, Michigan.
www.thomsonshore.com

Contents

Foreword

There was nothing understated about Jim Crow during that long, blistering century between the end of Reconstruction and the seminal legal victories of the American civil rights movement. Racist imagery essentializing blacks as inferior beings was as exaggerated as it was ubiquitous. The onslaught was constant.

Never mind that African Americans had only recently pulled off a miracle of human history, of enduring centuries of bondage to claim their freedom after a bloody four-year Civil War, many of them having served in the Union army and navy. After a brief decade of promise, there were, in Jim Crow's America, only lazy stereotypes to accompany the reassertion of white supremacy over black people depicted as guileless, shiftless, empty-headed, terrified, and conniving—clichés of clichés. Jim Crow's propaganda, stark and shocking, was designed to convince the American public—including blacks themselves—that they were all those things. It was exhausting: the pervasiveness of antiblack humor in newspapers, on store shelves, at the cinema, and along kitschy restaurant walls; Jim Crow's obsession with—and oversexualizing of—black bodies; and the frightening, gleaming delight those most committed to maintaining the color line in America took in policing the boundaries with the noose and gun and then posing for pictures with their victims' mutilated remains as if at a family picnic or barbecue.

No, there was nothing understated about Jim Crow.

Under-*standing* Jim Crow, however, is a different matter, with one question leading to countless others. How and why did de jure and de facto segregation evolve out of the unification of the country after the

Civil War, and why did it last for so long? How could anyone look at a real black person, of any period or station, and not see the shameful discrepancies between her or him and how black people, en masse, were portrayed in Jim Crow's America under the slanderous archetypes of "picaninny," "Tom," "Sambo," "coon," "Jezebel," "tragic mulatto," and "mammy"? Why *those* stereotypes and not others? Who masterminded them, what fantasies and fears were they projecting, and what were they trying to get others to buy? What were the real stakes involved? And when and how did African Americans take control of their own narrative, and the imagery needed to tell it, from silent film reels to "I Am a Man" signs, and fight back?

This is where David Pilgrim, the author of this book and founder of the Jim Crow Museum at Ferris State University in Big Rapids, Michigan, comes in. Reared in the Deep South during the tumultuous waning days of segregation—when a learned black professor at a Christian college still had to wear a chauffeur's hat to avoid unwanted attention driving his own car, bought with his own teacher's salary—Pilgrim channeled his anger in a way few would have thought of or dared. He began cornering the market on Jim Crow memorabilia, collecting with feverish intensity the odds and ends of the very system that had underwritten the racism he saw and felt everywhere around him.

Nothing was too trivial or disturbing for Pilgrim's net. Whereas most black kids coming of age in the 1960s and 1970s would have worked hard to block out the viciousness and cruelty depicted in vintage lynching postcards found in the shuffle, and turn off to the stock characters exaggeratedly drawn on brand-name cereal and soap boxes, Pilgrim opened his wallet, determined to buy up as much racist memorabilia as he could locate in order to confront—and, in doing so, master—the propaganda that accompanied the degradation of a people as they were emerging from centuries of slavery after the Civil War.

Then Pilgrim did something even more astonishing: he donated his entire collection, amassed over decades, to, of all places, a museum he founded at the university where he taught as a professor of sociology. Pilgrim's mission: to display in unflinching detail, and with the curatorial touch of a professional museum staff, the elaborate and dizzyingly extensive scaffolding of the Jim Crow system, as found in a breathtaking array of tangible objects, so that those coming of age as students and visitors behind him would not only not forget what *was* but be more vigilant about the residues that remain. Undergirding Pilgrim's mission was the powerful belief that we, as a society, heal better when we stare down the evils that have walked among us, together.

The truth is, the United States never had a truth and reconciliation commission after the Civil War (as post-Apartheid South Africa did) to air in the light of day the true nature and extent of the physical and psycho-logical traumas of slavery and segregation, both on the victims of those traumas and its perpetrators. Everyone, it seemed, was too busy moving forward, too anxious to move on, too shattered to heal in ways that could make a people and a nation whole. In his own way, then, David Pilgrim conceived of and built his Jim Crow Museum to function as just that: a truth and reconciliation commission, formed out of the detritus of Jim Crow, with an interpretive story encasing it that would help witnesses stare down the grotesqueries and, through a shared experience, con-front hard truths. That act of communal confrontation, Pilgrim believed, would lay the groundwork for "teaching tolerance and promoting social justice" from a humbler and more honest place.

It was a revolutionary idea.

Still, I have to admit I was uncertain about how I would feel visiting Pilgrim's Jim Crow Museum in the course of filming my PBS series, *The African Americans: Many Rivers to Cross*, in 2013. Even as a casual collec-tor of Jim Crow memorabilia myself (those of you who have visited The Hutchins Center for African and African American Research at Harvard know I am not shy about exploring our history in art or in defending every form of free speech against censorship), I wondered if anyone could effectively pull off an entire museum dedicated to its display and exorcism. And that was *before* I knew I would have to walk past a wall of glass behind which a whole family of Ku Klux Klan robes, for adults *and* children are cloaked on dummies! To say it was intense is a little like saying its gets chilly at the North Pole.

But then I realized that David Pilgrim had not merely displayed a collection of memorabilia; he had put the country itself on display during one of its most trying epochs, indeed what many consider the nadir of race relations in America. And in his staff's brilliant interpretation, we have, in this, the home of the largest collection of racist memorabilia in the country, the context for that nadir and a sense of how its tenta-cles continue to ensnare us and the politics of our time, from images of "welfare queens" to profiling by police to the first black president of the United States, all while the market for racist memorabilia continues to fetch huge sums from bidders online and at auction houses.

The renowned historian David Levering Lewis said to me on camera during the sequence in *Many Rivers to Cross* that highlighted the Jim Crow Museum, "Episode Four: Making a Way out of No Way (1897–1940)": "The African American in antebellum times was, as the stereotype held, reliable, faithful, hardworking, malleable. Indeed, one entrusted one's children, one's property to such people. Now, all of a sudden, the African American becomes demonized, a threat, a lascivious beast roaming the countryside of the South, people loosed by the end of slavery and now upon us like locusts. . . . Well, this was an absurdity." But it was an absurdity, we learn nearly every time we pick up a newspaper, which has lasted in various guises and in the most insidious ways, to this day. Pilgrim's approach to his museum was to create an experience that does anything *but* sweep these guises under the rug; instead, they are on full display.

Now, in his book *Understanding Jim Crow: Using Racist Memorabilia to Teach Tolerance and Promote Social Justice*, Pilgrim has bottled this museum experience up and bound it so that teachers and educators, not least general readers, can confront Jim Crow without having to travel all the way to Michigan. Equally fascinating and important are the behind-the-scenes stories Pilgrim offers about how he acquired his collection, and why, and what he learned about America along the way. There are remarkable stories in this book.

That doesn't mean it is easy. To run the gauntlet of memories, readers must turn past disgusting images of black babies as "Alligator Bait" and the painful, and pathetic, old carnival game "Hit the Coon." They must scan a "Nigger Milk" cartoon from 1916 and another cartoon showing a black man, in every exaggerated detail, absconding with a watermelon while a dog nips at his pants. Then they must stare at the various postcards Americans of the day bought and mailed to one another, fronted by ghastly lynching scenes and of "the Whipping Post." It is enough to turn the stomach several times.

Therefore, it is not surprising that there are those who worry Pilgrim's museum and book will unwittingly contribute to the brainwashing of would-be racists while coaxing the vulnerable to hate; that it will normalize violence through repetition; that, by inviting African Americans, particularly children, to *go there*, it will lead to the internalization of the very racist messages it is trying to eradicate, and, in doing so, deflate self-esteem; and that there can never be enough professorial context posted around the edges of the glass to protect us from the psychological ripple-effects of visiting such a ghoulish place. In short, the argument goes, if Jim Crow memorabilia was, as Stetson Kennedy once put it, fodder for a "Museum of Horrors," it would be wise to stay far away and suffocate it by ignoring it.

I understand that impulse, but I also understand that seeing is believing, and that through confronting the worst that has ever been said or depicted about us, new insights can emerge, along with new resolutions for action. There is, after all, a healing power in participating in communal experiences steeped in sadness that cannot—and must not—be overlooked. Repression, conversely, robs us of a vocabulary for what we know is wrong, allowing feelings to "fester" or "explode," to borrow from the Langston Hughes poem "Harlem," which inspired the classic Lorraine Hansberry play *A Raisin in the Sun*. Instead, by confronting our fears, we learn to master them, and from that learning comes the wisdom to see a nemesis like Jim Crow for what it really was—a systematic attempt to undermine a people by framing, and justifying, their second-class status *before* they could fulfill the promises of citizenship under a Constitution that previously had considered them property. In that light, there is a pride that comes from walking through the Jim Crow Museum knowing all we have accomplished as a people in the face of such an onslaught. As poignant, in absorbing the weight of that onslaught, we gain a much deeper appreciation for not only the monumental heroes of African American history but the everyday heroes who "made a way out of no way" by marrying, raising families, keeping down a job, riding a bus, attending a church, knowing full well that any day could be *the* day when terrorism, stoked by the racist imagery we see everywhere on display, arrived at their door. Make no mistake: that terror was real for black families who lived in Jim Crow America, and it remains real in memories that continue to haunt and wound, as evidenced by the June 2015 mass shooting at the Emanuel AME Church in Charleston, South Carolina.

In his introduction to this book, Pilgrim likens himself to a "garbage collector," and there is a certain truth in that. I prefer to think of him as a battlefield collector, for every manifestation of Jim Crow, whether through imagery or violence, was a battle with the potential to wound or kill. David Pilgrim has dedicated his life to walking those battlefields— the auction houses, pawn shops, garage sales, and backroom collections of America—and in amassing his unique and unprecedented storehouse of racist memorabilia, he has provided totalizing proof that the war was real and that its legacy is enduring whether we choose to confront it or not.

I hope your confrontation will begin in these pages.

Henry Louis Gates Jr.
Alphonse Fletcher University Professor, Harvard University
Cambridge, Massachusetts
June 25, 2015

Acknowledgments

I am indebted to the people who helped with the research and preparation of this manuscript: Neil Baumgartner, Franklin Hughes, Lisa Kemmis, Michael Maxson, Fran Rosen, and Patty Terryn. And I am grateful to my family for their patience and support: Margaret Elizabeth, Haley Grace, Gabrielle Lynne, and Eustace Jamison. Finally, I am proud to work at Ferris State University in Big Rapids, Michigan, one of the few institutions courageous enough to build a Jim Crow Museum.

CHAPTER ONE

The Garbage Man: Why I Collect Racist Objects

As for me, I raced around the dumpsters collecting discarded "White" and "Colored" signs, thinking they would be of some interest to posterity in a Museum of Horrors.

—Stetson Kennedy[1]

I am a garbage collector—racist garbage. For three decades I collected items that defame and belittle Africans and their American descendants. I have a parlor game, *72 Pictured Party Stunts*, from the 1930s. One of the game's cards instructs players to "go through the motions of a colored boy eating watermelon." The card shows a dark black boy, with bulging eyes and blood-red lips, eating a watermelon as large as he is. The card offends me, but I collected it and thousands of similar items that portray blacks as coons, Toms, Sambos, mammies, picaninnies, and other dehumanizing racial caricatures. I collect this garbage because I believe, and know to be true, that items of intolerance can be used to teach tolerance and promote social justice.

I bought my first racist object when I was twelve or thirteen. My memory of that event is not perfect. It was the early 1970s in Mobile, Alabama, the home of my youth. The item was small, probably a mammy saltshaker. It must have been cheap because I never had much money. And it must have been ugly, because after I paid the dealer I threw the item to the ground, shattering it. It was not a political act; I simply hated it, if you can hate an object. I do not know if he scolded me, he almost certainly did. I was what folks in Mobile, blacks and whites, indelicately referred to as a "Red Nigger"—a pejorative term for light-skinned African

NIGGER MILK

Americans. In those days, in that place, he could have thrown that name at me, without incident. I do not remember what he called me, but I am certain he called me something other than David Pilgrim.

I have a 1916 magazine advertisement that shows a little black boy, softly caricatured, drinking from an ink bottle. The bottom caption reads, "Nigger Milk." I bought the print in 1988 from an antique store in La Porte, Indiana. It was framed and offered for sale at twenty dollars. The sales clerk wrote "Black Print" on the receipt. I told her to write, "Nigger Milk Print." And, I added, "If you are going to sell it, call it by its name." She refused. We argued. I bought the print and left. That was my last argument with a dealer or sales clerk; today, I purchase the items and leave with little or no conversation.

The mammy saltshaker and the "Nigger Milk" print are not the most offensive items that I have seen. In 1874, McLoughlin Brothers of New York manufactured a puzzle game called "Chopped Up Niggers." Today, it is a prized collectible. I have twice seen the game for sale, but neither time did I have the $3,000 necessary to purchase it.[2] There are postcards from the first half of the twentieth century that show blacks being whipped, or worse, hanging dead from trees, or lying on the ground burned beyond

LEFT: The "Nigger Milk" cartoon was relatively common through the 1920s. **ABOVE:** These Mammy objects are similar to the first one I purchased—and destroyed.

recognition. Postcards and photographs of lynched blacks sell for around $400 each on eBay and other internet auction houses. I can afford to buy one, but I am not ready, not yet.

My friends claim that I am obsessed with racist objects. If they are right, the obsession began while I was an undergraduate student at Jarvis Christian College, a small historically black institution in Hawkins, Texas. The teachers taught more than scientific principles and mathematical equations. I learned from them what it was like to live as a black man under Jim Crow segregation. Imagine being a college professor but having to wear a chauffeur's hat while driving your new car through small towns, lest some disgruntled white man beat you for being "uppity." The stories I heard were not angry ones; no, worse, they were matter-of-fact accounts of everyday life in a land where every black person was considered inferior to every white person, a time when "social equality" was a profane expression, fighting words. Blacks knew their clothing sizes. Why? They were not allowed to try on clothes in department stores. If blacks and whites wore the same clothes, even for a short while, it implied social equality and, perhaps, intimacy.

I was ten years old when Martin Luther King Jr. was killed; we watched the funeral on a small black and white television in my fifth-grade class at Bessie C. Fonville Elementary School. All my classmates were black; Mobile was proudly, defiantly segregated. Two years later, in search of a cheaper house, my family moved to Prichard, Alabama, a small adjoining city that was even more segregated. Less than a decade earlier, blacks had not been allowed to use the Prichard Public Library unless they had a note from a white person. Whites owned most of the stores and held all the elected offices. I was part of the class that integrated Prichard Middle School. A local television commentator called it an "invasion." Invaders? We were children. We fought adult whites on the way to school and white children at school. By the time I graduated from Mattie T. Blount High School, most of the whites had left the city. When I arrived at Jarvis Christian College I was not naive about southern race relations.

My college teachers taught the usual lessons about Frederick Douglass, Sojourner Truth, Booker T. Washington, and W.E.B. Du Bois. More importantly, they taught about the daily heroism of the maids, butlers, and sharecroppers who risked their jobs, and sometimes their lives, to protest Jim Crow segregation. I learned to read history critically, from the "bottom up," not as a linear critique of so-called great men, but from the viewpoint of oppressed people. I realized the great debt that I owed to the blacks—all but a few forgotten by history—who suffered so that I could be educated. It was at Jarvis Christian College that I learned

that a scholar could be an activist, indeed must be. Here, I first had the idea of building a collection of racist objects. I was not sure what I would do with it.

All racial groups have been caricatured in this country, but none have been caricatured as often or in as many ways as have black Americans. Blacks have been portrayed in popular culture as pitiable exotics, cannibalistic savages, hypersexual deviants, childlike buffoons, obedient servants, self-loathing victims, and menaces to society. These antiblack depictions were routinely manifested in or on material objects: ashtrays, drinking glasses, banks, games, fishing lures, detergent boxes, and other everyday items. These objects both reflected and shaped attitudes toward African Americans. Robbin Henderson, former director of the Berkeley Art Center, said, "Derogatory imagery enables people to absorb stereotypes; which in turn allows them to ignore and condone injustice, discrimination, segregation, and racism."[3] She was right. Racist imagery is propaganda, and that propaganda was used to support Jim Crow laws and customs.

Jim Crow was more than a series of "Whites Only" signs. It was a way of life that approximated a racial caste system.[4] Jim Crow laws and etiquette were aided by millions of material objects that portrayed blacks

ABOVE: Each year thousands of people visit the museum.
OVERLEAF: No group has been caricatured as often in as many ways as have African Americans.

Caricaturing Bl

THE NEGRO A BEAST

IN THE IMAGE OF GOD

From the collection of the Jim Crow Museum.

In the United
groups have b
but none as of
ways as black
have been port
culture as pitia
cannibalistic sa
deviants, childl
obedient servan
victims, and me

These anti-black depictions routinely took
objects, such as ashtrays, drinking glasses, b
fishing lures, detergent boxes, and other eve
This case holds objects that illustrate some o
anti-black caricatures.

BOARD of TRADE
CHEWING
TOBACCO

Uncle Remus

25 OUNCES
FOR
25¢

Liberty

THEY SHO' MAKE YOU FEEL
AT HOME HERE!

WELCOME

SHREVE, OHIO

Tom

"TEN LITTLE NIGGER BOYS WENT OUT TO DINE"

as laughable, detestable inferiors. The coon caricature, for example, described black men as lazy, easily frightened, chronically idle, inarticulate, physically ugly idiots. This distorted representation of black men found its way onto postcards, sheet music, children's games, and many other material objects. The coon and other stereotypical images buttressed the view that blacks were unfit to attend racially integrated schools, live in safe neighborhoods, work in responsible jobs, vote, and hold public office. With little effort I can hear the voices of my black elders—parents, neighbors, teachers—demanding, almost pleading, "Don't be coon, be a man." Living under Jim Crow meant battling shame.

I collected many racist objects during my four years as a graduate student at the Ohio State University. Most of the items were small and inexpensive. I paid two dollars for a postcard that showed a terrified black man being eaten by an alligator. I paid five dollars for a matchbook that showed a Sambo-like character with oversized genitalia. The collection that I amassed was not a sample of what existed in Ohio—or any state; it was, instead, a sample of what I could afford. Brutally racist items were, and remain, the most expensive "black collectibles." In Orrville, Ohio, I saw a framed print showing naked black children climbing a fence to enter a swimming hole. The caption read, "Last One In's A Nigger." I did not have the $125 to purchase it. That was the early 1980s, a few years before the prices for racist collectibles escalated. Today, that print, if authentic, sells for several thousand dollars. On vacation, I scoured flea markets and antique stores from Ohio to Alabama, looking for items that denigrated black people.

My years at Ohio State were, I realize now, filled with much anger. I suppose every sane black person must be angry—for a while. I was in the Sociology Department, a politically liberal department, and talk about improving race relations was common. There were five or six black students, and we clung together like frightened outsiders. I will not speak for my black colleagues, but I was sincerely doubtful of my white professors' understanding of everyday racism. Their lectures were often brilliant, but never complete. Race relations were fodder for theoretical debate; blacks were a "research category." Real blacks, with real ambitions and problems, were problematic. I was suspicious of my white teachers and several reciprocated that feeling.

A friend suggested that I take some of my elective courses in the Black Studies Program. I did. James Upton, a political scientist, introduced me to Paul Robeson's book *Here I Stand*.[5] Robeson, an accomplished athlete and entertainer, was also an activist who believed that American capitalism was pernicious and detrimental to poor people, especially black Americans. Robeson maintained his political convictions despite

TOP: These "Jolly Nigger" banks were made throughout the late nineteenth and early twentieth centuries. They are caricatured representations of "nigger minstrels."
BOTTOM: During the Jim Crow period it was not unusual for Americans to name their darkly colored pets "Nigger."

9

Show how a hungry
colored boy would go
for roast chicken.

Go through the motions
of a colored boy eating
watermelon.

ostracism and outright persecution. I was not anticapitalist, but I admired his willingness to follow his political convictions—and his unwavering fight for the rights of oppressed people. I read many books about race and race relations but few impacted me as much as *Here I Stand*. I read James Baldwin's novels and essays. His anger found a willing ear, but I was troubled by his homosexuality. That is hardly surprising. I was reared in a community that was demonstratively homophobic. Homosexuality was seen as weakness, and "sissies" were "bad luck." White bigots do not have a monopoly on ignorance. Progressiveness is a journey. I had a long way to go.

I have long felt that Americans, especially whites, would rather talk about slavery than Jim Crow. All ex-slaves are dead. They do not walk among us, their presence a reminder of that unspeakably cruel system. Their children are dead. Distanced by a century and a half, the modern American sees slavery as a regrettable period when blacks worked without wages. Slavery was, of course, much worse. It was the complete domination of one people by another people—with the expected abuses that accompany unchecked power. Slavers whipped slaves who displeased

Cards from "72 Pictured Party Stunts," a 1930s parlor game.

them. Clergy preached that slavery was the will of God. Scientists "proved" that blacks were less evolved, a subspecies of the human race. Politicians agreed. Teachers taught young children that blacks were inherently less intelligent. Laws forbade slaves, and sometimes free blacks, from reading, writing, owning money, and arguing with whites. Slaves were property— thinking, suffering property. The passing of a century and a half affords the typical American enough psychological space to deal with slavery; when that is not sufficient, a sanitized version of slavery is embraced.

The horrors of Jim Crow are not so easily ignored. The children of Jim Crow walk among us, and they have stories to tell. They remember Emmett Till, murdered in 1955 for flirting with a white woman. Long before the tragic bombings of September 11, 2001, blacks who lived under Jim Crow were acquainted with terrorism. On Sunday, September 15, 1963, the Sixteenth Street Baptist Church, a black church in Birmingham, Alabama, was bombed. Twenty-three people were hurt, and four girls were killed.[6] The blacks who grew up during the Jim Crow period can tell you about this bombing and many other acts of domestic terrorism. Blacks who dared protest the indignities of Jim Crow were threatened

The Gold Dust Twin characters of *Goldie* and *Dustie* were the "faces" of Gold Dust washing products and became one of the earliest brand-driven trademarks in American advertising.

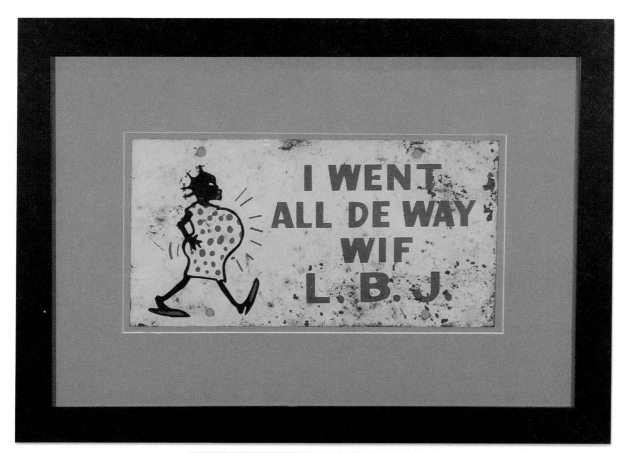

and, when the threats did not work, subjected to violence, including bombings. The children of Jim Crow can talk about the Scottsboro boys, the Tuskegee experiment, lynching, and the assassination of Martin Luther King Jr., and they have stories about the daily indignities that befell blacks who lived in towns where they were not respected or wanted.

Yes, many of us would rather talk about slavery than Jim Crow because a discussion of Jim Crow raises the question, "What about today?"

In 1990 I joined the sociology faculty at Ferris State University in Big Rapids, Michigan. At that time, my collection of racist artifacts numbered more than a thousand. I kept the collection in my home, bringing out pieces when I gave public addresses, mainly to high school students. I discovered that many young people, blacks and whites, were not only ignorant about historical expressions of racism, but they believed that I was exaggerating when I described the awfulness of Jim Crow. Their ignorance disappointed me. I showed them segregation signs, Ku Klux Klan robes, and everyday objects that portrayed blacks with ragged clothes, unkempt hair, bulging eyes, and clown-like lips—running toward fried chicken and watermelons and running away from alligators. I talked to the students about the connection between Jim Crow laws and racist material objects. I was too heavy-handed, too driven to make them understand; I was learning to use the objects as teaching tools—while, simultaneously, dealing with my anger.

A seminal event occurred in 1991. A colleague told me about an elderly black woman who had a large collection of black-related objects. I will call her Mrs. Haley. She was an antique dealer in a small town. I visited her and told her about my collection. She seemed unimpressed. I described how I used the racist objects to teach students about racism. Again, she was not impressed. Her store displayed a few pieces of racist memorabilia. I asked if she kept most of the "black material" at her home. She said that she kept those pieces in the back, but I could only see them if I agreed to a condition, namely, I could never "pester" her to sell me any of the objects. I agreed. She locked the front door, put the "closed" sign in the window, and motioned for me to follow her.

If I live to be a hundred, I will never forget the feeling that I had when I saw her collection; it was sadness, a thick, cold sadness. There were hundreds, maybe thousands, of objects, side by side, on shelves that reached to the ceiling. All four walls were covered with the most racist objects imaginable. I owned some of the objects, others I had seen in black memorabilia price guides, and others were so rare I have not seen them since. I was stunned. Sadness. It was as if I could hear the pieces talking, yowling. Every conceivable distortion of black people, our people, was on display. It was a chamber of horrors. She did not talk. She stared

TOP: License plate from the 1960s mocking Lyndon B. Johnson's presidential campaign slogan, "All the Way with L.B.J."
BOTTOM: This is one of the many segregation signs that were common during the Jim Crow era. *No Niggers, No Jews, No Dogs* (2000) is also the name of a play by John Henry Redwood. Set in Halifax, North Carolina, in the late 1940s, it dramatizes the victimization of an African American family.

at me; I stared at the objects. One was a life-sized wooden figure of a black man, grotesquely caricatured. It was a testament to the creative energy that often lurks behind racism. On her shelves was a material record of all the hurt and harm done to Africans and their American descendants. I wanted to cry. It was at that moment that I decided to create a museum.

I visited her often. She liked me because I was "from down home." She told me that in the 1960s and 1970s many whites gave her racist objects. They did not want to be identified with racism. They were embarrassed. That sentiment changed in the mid-1980s. Several price guides devoted solely to racist collectibles were published. The price guides helped create the contemporary market for racist collectibles. Each new price guide showed prices escalating, and a national pursuit of racist items ensued. Mrs. Haley's collection was worth hundreds of thousands of dollars, but she had no desire to sell the pieces. They were our past, America's past. "We mustn't forget, baby," she said, without even a hint of anger. I stopped visiting after a year or so, she died, and I heard that her collection was sold to private dealers. That broke my heart on several levels. It bothers me that she did not live to see the museum she helped inspire.

I continued to collect racist objects: musical records with racist themes, fishing lures with Sambo imagery, children's games that showed naked, dirty black children—any and every racist item that I could afford. In the cold months I bought from antique stores; in the warmer months, I traveled to flea markets. I was impatient. I sought to purchase entire collections from dealers and collectors. Again, limited finances restricted me to purchasing only small collections.

In 1994 I was part of a three-person team from Ferris State University that attended a two-week workshop at Colorado College in Colorado Springs. The conference, sponsored by the Lilly Foundation, was devoted to the liberal arts. The charge to our team was to introduce diversity into the general education curriculum at Ferris State University. I traveled with Mary Murnik, a colleague, to all the local antique stores. Colorado Springs is a politically conservative city; not surprisingly, there were many racist items for sale—some vintage, many reproductions. I bought several segregation signs, a Coon Chicken Inn glass, three racist ashtrays, and many other items. I also bought several 1920s records, all with racist themes, from a dealer who tried to talk about "the problem with colored people." I wanted the records; I did not want the conversation. John Thorp, the other member of the team, and I spent hours planning a strategy to convince the Ferris State University administration to give physical space and money to a room that would house my racist collectibles.

In 1996, the Jim Crow Museum of Racist Memorabilia opened at Ferris State University. The room was small, only five hundred square

feet, and, to be honest, it was more visual storage than an actual museum. But it was a start. I donated my entire collection to the university, with the condition that the objects would be displayed and preserved. Most collectors are soothed by their collections, but I hated mine and was relieved to get it out of my home. I never liked having the objects in my home. I had small children. They would wander to the basement and look at "daddy's dolls"—two mannequins dressed in full Ku Klux Klan regalia.

One of many early 1900s games that used black Americans as targets.

They played with the racist target games. One of them, I do not know which, broke a "Tom" cookie jar. I was angry for two days. The irony is not lost to me.

Ferris State University faculty and students used the museum to understand historical and contemporary expressions of racism. The museum included items created after the Jim Crow period ended; this was a valuable addition because too many students dismiss racism as a relic of the past. Scholars conducting research, mainly social scientists, also visited the museum. Only rarely were children allowed in the room and adults—preferably their parents—were encouraged to accompany them. We encouraged visitors to watch Marlon Riggs's documentary *Ethnic Notions* or *Jim Crow's Museum*—a documentary I produced and Clayton Rye directed—before entering the room.[7] A trained museum facilitator was there for all tours. Clergy, civil rights groups, and human rights organizations also visited the museum.

The mission of the Jim Crow Museum is straightforward: to use items of intolerance to teach tolerance and promote social justice. We examine the historical patterns of race relations and the origins and consequences of racist depictions. The aim is to engage visitors in open and honest dialogues about this country's racial history. We are not afraid to talk about race and racism; we are afraid not to have these conversations. I continue to deliver public presentations at high schools and colleges. Race relations suffer when discussions of race and racism are verboten. High schools that sincerely include race, racism, and diversity in their curriculums increase tolerance for others. It is relatively easy to identify those high schools that are afraid of or unwilling to honestly examine race and racism. There you will find a 1950s-like pattern of everyday

This is a paper sign that was used in the 1920s to advertise for rock breakers. Riprap is rock or other material used to armor shoreline structures against water or ice erosion.

racism. Racial stereotypes will dominate, though they may go unspoken. Inevitably, there will be a racial incident—a racial slur hurled, a fight blamed on "the other," and, with no relevant foundation laid for dealing with the problem, the school hires me or a similar "diversity consultant" to restore order. But nothing changes. The Jim Crow Museum is founded on the belief that open, honest, even painful discussions about race are necessary to avoid repeating yesterday's mistakes.

Our goal is not to shock visitors. A thick naiveté about the racial past permeates this country. Many Americans understand historical racism mainly as a general abstraction: Racism existed; it was bad, though probably not as bad as blacks and other minorities claim. A confrontation with the visual evidence of racism—especially thousands of items in a small space—is frequently shocking, even agonizing. In the late 1800s traveling carnivals and amusement parks sometimes included a game called African Dodger. A black man would stick his head through a hole in a painted canvas; the background was typically a plantation scene. White patrons threw balls—and, in especially brutal instances, rocks—at the black man's head to win prizes. A person living in the twenty-first century who sees that banner or a reproduction gets a glimpse of what it was like to be a black man in the early years of Jim Crow.

That carnival banner reinforced the idea that blacks were not as human as whites. It alleviated white guilt about black pain; it suggested that blacks did not experience pain the way normal people—meaning whites—experienced pain. It helped legitimize "happy violence" directed against blacks. It functioned as an ego massage for the white hurlers. How many poorly paid, socially marginalized whites expressed their frustration at the expense of black heads? The African Dodger game and its cousin, Hit the Coon, were eventually replaced with target games that used wooden black heads. You do not have to be a psychologist to understand the symbolic violence. Not coincidentally, games that used blacks as targets were popular when the lynching of real blacks was common. The Jim Crow Museum now includes a recreation of the African Dodger game and many other objects that show blacks being thrown at, hit, or beaten.

Some Truths Are Painful

Anger is a necessary leg on many journeys, but it cannot be the destination. My anger reached its apex when I read *The Turner Diaries*, written by William L. Pierce using the pen name Andrew Macdonald.[8] The book chronicles the "heroism" of white supremacists who overthrow the federal government, win a bloody race war, and establish a social order where whites rule. Blacks, other minorities, and the whites who support them

ALLIGATOR BAIT.

Looks rather Tuff

are brutally, graphically killed. This book, arguably the most racist book produced in the second half of the twentieth century, has influenced numerous racist organizations, including The Order and The Aryan Republican Army. Timothy McVeigh, convicted of the 1995 bombing of the Federal Building in Oklahoma City, was a fan of the book, and his bombing was similar to bombings described in *The Turner Diaries*. I made the mistake of reading it—all eighty thousand words—in one day, while I was tired. It consumed me.

Pierce, who held a PhD in physics from the University of Colorado, bonded with Nazis in the 1960s. That explains why he wrote the book, but why did it anger me so much? I had, after all, a basement full of racist memorabilia. I was raised in the segregated South. I remember the race riots on Davis Avenue in Mobile, Alabama. I was familiar with the many ways that you can call me a nigger and threaten to hurt me. The ideas in Pierce's book, though venomous, were not new to me. Yet that book shook me.[9]

After that time, I took a colleague's students into the Jim Crow Museum. I showed them the ugliness, the mammy, the Sambo, the brute, the caricatured sores foisted on black Americans. I showed them. Showed it all. And we went deep, deeper than ever before, deeper than I meant

This 1920s postcard is a variant of a 1896 print.

to go. My anger showed. After three hours they left, all but two—a young black woman and a middle-aged white man. The woman sat, paralyzed, transfixed, and stunned before a picture of five naked black children. The children sat on a riverbank. At the bottom of the picture were these words: "Alligator Bait." She sat there, watching it, trying to understand the hand that had made it, the mind that conceived it. She did not say a word, but her eyes, her frown, the hand at her forehead all said, "Why, sweet Jesus, why?" The white man stopped staring at the items and looked at me. He was crying. Not a sob, a single tear stream. His tears moved me. I walked toward him. Before I could talk, he said, "I am sorry, Mr. Pilgrim. Please forgive me."

He had not created the racist objects in the room, but he had benefited from living in a society where blacks were oppressed. Racial healing follows sincere contrition. I never realized how much I needed to hear some white person, any sincere white person, say, "I am sorry, forgive me." I wanted and needed an apology—a heartfelt one that changes two lives. His words took the steam out of my anger. The Jim Crow Museum was not created to shock, shame, or anger, but to lead to a deeper understanding of the historical racial divide. Some visitors to the museum say that I seem so detached; I am not. I have struggled to harness my anger and channel it into productive work.

Most people who visit the Jim Crow Museum understand our mission, accept our methods, and continue the journey toward understanding and improving race relations. But we have critics. That is to be expected. The twenty-first century has brought a fear and unwillingness to look at racism in a deep, systematic manner. The hedonistic desire to avoid pain (or anything uncomfortable) is counter to our method of directly confronting the ugly legacy of racism. Moreover, there is a growing desire among many Americans to forget the past and move forward. "If we just stop talking about historical racism, racism will go away." It is not that easy. We may not talk openly about race, but that is not forgetting it. The United States remains a nation residentially segregated by race. Our churches, temples, and synagogues are, in the main, racially divided. Old patterns of racial segregation have returned to many public schools. Race matters. Racial stereotypes, sometimes yelled, sometimes whispered, are common. Overt racism has morphed into institutional racism, symbolic racism, and everyday racialism. Attitudes and beliefs about race inform many of our decisions, big and small. "Let's stop talking about it" is a plea for comfort—a comfort denied to blacks and other minorities. The way to move forward is to confront the historical and the contemporary expressions of racism, and to do so in a setting where attitudes, values, and behaviors are intelligently and civilly critiqued.

Although a docent is always present, the museum was designed to accommodate self-tours.

The Jim Crow Museum is, in effect, a black holocaust museum. I mean no disrespect to the millions of Jews and others who died at the hands of the maniacal Adolf Hitler and his followers. I hesitate to use the word *holocaust* to describe the experiences of Africans and their American descendants because I do not want to trivialize the suffering of Jews, nor do I want to compare victimizations. But what word should I use? Thousands of Africans died during the trans-Atlantic slave voyage. Millions lived under the brutal system of slavery, and even after slavery was officially ended thousands of blacks were lynched—many ritualistically, by white mobs. We have today many small "white towns" that were created because the blacks were driven out, victims of wanton racial violence. Yes, Africans and their American descendants experienced a holocaust in this country.

In 2012, the Jim Crow Museum moved into a larger facility, which allowed additional stories to be told. Artifacts and signage introduce visitors to the wonderful accomplishments of black artists, scholars, scientists, inventors, politicians, military personnel, and athletes who thrived despite living under Jim Crow. Also, a civil rights movement section was added. There, visitors find images of protesters with a sign, "I, Too, Am A Man." Visitors learn about the civil rights workers, many not commonly found in history books. This section can be conceptualized as a "Death of de jure Jim Crow" space, though, truth be told, vestiges of Jim Crow–era

thinking remain. This is evident by the large display of racist objects produced since 2000.

The new museum has a room of reflection. In that room is a mural called "Cloud of Witnesses." It includes the portraits of many people, blacks and whites, who gave their lives during the civil rights movement. The mural surrounds visitors in the room of reflection. It is a perfect backdrop to the question, "What can I do today to address racism?" The mural was painted by Jon McDonald, a talented artist from Kendall College of Art and Design of Ferris State University. In 2012, Malaak Shabazz, the daughter of Malcolm X, visited the museum. It brought tears to my eyes when she said that McDonald's portrait of her father on the mural would have made her mother, Betty Shabazz, proud.

Jim Crow was wounded in the 1950s and 1960s. The Supreme Court's decision in *Brown v. Board of Education of Topeka, Kansas* (1954) ruled segregated schools unconstitutional. This hastened the end of legal segregation, but it did not end it, as evidenced by the need for the civil rights movement. Whites, especially northerners, were confronted with images of black protesters being beaten by police officers, attacked by police dogs, and arrested for trying to vote, eat at segregated lunch counters, and attend "white" schools. The 1964 Civil Rights Act, passed after (and maybe because of) President John F. Kennedy's death, was certainly a blow to Jim Crow.

Malaak Shabazz, daughter of slain civil rights leader Malcolm X, visited the museum in 2012.

One by one, segregation laws were removed in the 1960s and 1970s. The elimination of legal barriers to voting led to the election of black politicians in many cities, including former bastions of segregation such as Birmingham and Atlanta. From this period forward, white colleges and universities in the South admitted black students, and hired black professors, albeit often a token number. Affirmative action programs forced employers in both the public and private sectors to hire blacks and other minorities. Some blacks appeared on television shows in nonstereotypical ways. Significant racial problems remained but it seemed that Jim Crow–era attitudes and behaviors were destined to die. Many whites destroyed their household items that defamed black people, for example, ashtrays with smiling Sambos, "Jolly Nigger" banks, sheet music with titles like "Coon, Coon, Coon," and children's books like *Little Black Sambo*.

Jim Crow attitudes did not die. The end of the twentieth century found many whites resentful of gains by blacks. Affirmative action policies were attacked as reverse discrimination against whites. The slavery-era coon caricature of blacks as lazy, ne'er-do-wells reemerged as caricatures of modern welfare recipients. White Americans support welfare for the "deserving poor" but strongly oppose it for persons perceived as lazy and unwilling to work. Black welfare recipients are seen as indolent parasites. The centuries-old fear of blacks, especially young black males, as brutes found new life in contemporary portrayals of blacks as thugs, gangsters, and menaces to society.

Black entertainers who capitalize financially on white America's acceptance of antiblack stereotypes perpetuate many of these images. In popular and material culture, the mammy portrayal of black women was replaced by the Jezebel image: black women as hypersexual deviants. The racial sensitivity that had been promoted in the 1970s and 1980s was by the end of the century derided as political correctness.

The new racial climate is marked by ambivalence and contradiction. The 2008 election of Barack Obama, a multiracial, black-identified man, as president represents significant racial progress for the nation—and his reelection in 2012 has led some Americans to prematurely claim that we have entered a postracial era. There is a heightened sense that racism is wrong and that tolerating "racial others" is good, but there remains an acceptance of ideas critical of and belittling toward blacks and other minorities. Many whites are tired of talking about race, believing that America has made enough "concessions" to its black citizens. Some are rebelling against government intrusion, arguing that the government, especially the federal government, does not have the right to force integration. Still others wage personal battles against political correctness. And then there is that segment of the white population that still believes

This postcard, postmarked 1907, typifies the Sambo portrayal: lazy, irresponsible, and childlike.

Sambo

that blacks are less intelligent, less ambitious, less moral, and more given to social pathological behaviors: drug abuse, sexual deviance, and crimes against property and persons. Martin Luther King Jr., vilified during his life, is hailed as a hero. Blacks as a whole are too frequently viewed with suspicion, sometimes alarm.

In the early 1990s I attended an academic conference in New Orleans. I searched local stores for racist objects. There were not many. Ten years later I returned to New Orleans. I found antiblack objects in many stores. This is disappointing but not unexpected. Brutally racist items are readily available through internet auction houses, most notably eBay. Indeed, practically every item housed in the Jim Crow Museum is being sold on some internet site. Old racist items are being reproduced and new items are being created.

In 2003, David Chang created a national uproar with his game, Ghettopoly. Unlike Monopoly, the popular family game, Ghettopoly debases and belittles racial minorities, especially blacks. Ghettopoly has seven game pieces: Pimp, Hoe, 40 oz., Machine Gun, Marijuana Leaf, Basketball, and Crack. One of the game's cards reads, "You got yo whole neighborhood addicted to crack. Collect $50 from each playa." Monopoly has houses and hotels; Ghettopoly has crack houses and projects. The distributors advertise Ghettopoly this way: "Buying stolen properties, pimpin hoes, building crack houses and projects, paying protection fees and getting car jacked are some of the elements of the game. Not dope enough? If you don't have the money that you owe to the loan shark you might just land yourself in da Emergency Room." The game's cards depict blacks in physically caricatured ways. Hasbro, the owner of the copyright for Monopoly, sued David Chang to make him stop distributing Ghettopoly.

David Chang promoted his product as a satirical critique of American racism. He is not alone. AdultDolls.net is the distributor of Trash Talker Dolls, a set of dolls with stereotypical depictions of minorities. Their best seller is Pimp Daddy, a chain-wearing, gaudily dressed, black pimp who says, among other things, "You better make some money, bitch." Charles Knipp, a white man, has gained national notoriety for his minstrel-drag "Ignunce Tour." Knipp, dressed in ragged women's clothes and blackface makeup, adopts the stage persona Shirley Q. Liquor—a coon-like black woman with nineteen children. This self-proclaimed "Queen of Dixie" has many skits, each portraying blacks as buffoons, whores, idlers, and crooks. While Knipp's performances are popular in the Deep South, he has been protested in many northern cities.[10] Shirley Q. Liquor collectibles, including cassette tapes, drinking glasses, and posters are popular. When satire does not work, it promotes the thing satirized. Ghettopoly, Trash Talker Dolls, and Shirley Q. Liquor skits and products portray blacks as

immoral, wretched, ill-bred, cultural parasites. These modern depictions of blacks are reminiscent of the negative caricatures found more than a century ago. The satire does not work but the distributors get paid.

The Jim Crow Museum website (www.ferris.edu/jimcrow) has a feature called ". . . and it doesn't stop." A perusal of the material on that space clearly demonstrates that new racially tinged and blatantly racist objects are still being created. For example, in 2012 there were shooting targets created that depicted Trayvon Martin, the young African American whose killing made national news.

Understanding is the principal thing. The museum's holdings force visitors to take a stand for or against the equality of all people. It works. I have witnessed deep and honest discussions about race and racism. No topics are forbidden. What role have blacks played in perpetuating antiblack caricatures and stereotypes? When, if ever, is folk art racially offensive? Is segregation along racial lines always indicative of racism?

This dart target "book" has no date.

25

We analyze the origins and consequences of racist imagery, but we do not stop there.

I am humbled that the Jim Crow Museum has become a national resource—and the museum's website an international resource. The website was created by Ted Halm, the Ferris State University webmaster. Franklin Hughes revamped the website in 2011. Two dozen Ferris State University faculty have been trained to function as docents, leading tours and facilitating discussions about the objects. Traveling exhibits carry the museum's lessons to other universities and colleges. The museum has had two directors, John Thorp and Andy Karafa, and both served with distinction. The museum is a team effort. A vision without help is a cathartic dream.

I see my role as decreasing. I have other goals, other garbage to collect. I have collected several hundred objects that defame and belittle women—items that both reflected and shaped negative attitudes toward women. I am now building a room, modeled after the Jim Crow Museum, that uses sexist objects to teach Americans to better understand sexism. Martin Luther King Jr. said, "Injustice anywhere is a threat to justice everywhere." In 2004, Carrie Stirmer, the director of the Ferris Art Gallery, and I designed and built a traveling exhibit called *Hateful Things*. This exhibit has traveled to many universities and museums teaching about the horrors of Jim Crow segregation. In 2005 we built "Them: Images of Separation," a traveling exhibit that focuses on material objects that defame blacks, women, Asians, Jews, Mexicans, gays, and poor whites. Again, our goal is to use items of intolerance to teach tolerance.

The mission and tagline of the museum is "Using Objects of Intolerance to Teach Tolerance." Although most people support our mission as written, there have always been people troubled by our use of the word *tolerance*. For example, at a recent National Conference on Race & Ethnicity in American Higher Education, several participants described it as a weak, wimpy word. They demanded, in voices loud and clear, to be accepted not tolerated. They found the word to represent a low bar. For them, it meant putting up with something or someone that you find—actually or potentially—unpleasant, disagreeable, or too different.

The word *tolerance* has multiple meanings. It can, as implied above, mean "the capacity or willingness to endure something, especially pain, hardship, or difference." But it has another meaning: "the willingness to recognize and respect the beliefs or practices of others." This latter definition is consistent with the mission of the Jim Crow Museum. Our conception of tolerance is similar to the one developed by the United Nations Educational, Scientific and Cultural Organization (UNESCO), which stated, "Tolerance is respect, acceptance and appreciation of the rich diversity of our world's cultures, our forms of expression and ways of being human. Tolerance is harmony in difference." From my perspective, tolerance and acceptance are not competing words or ideas. Rather, I have viewed (or conceptualized) tolerance as an umbrella term that includes acceptance.

Words fall out of favor. When was the last time you heard someone use the term *racial integration*? I remember when people who do the work we do used the terms *pluralism* and *multiculturalism*. Today, those words seem out of date, quaint. They were replaced with the word *diversity*, which itself is giving way to the term *inclusion*. And, there are only seven people in the entire nation who regularly use the word *desegregation*—I am one of them. It is apparent that *tolerance* is falling or has already fallen out of favor with my progressive colleagues.

There are no perfect thoughts; there are no perfect words to reflect thoughts. We have and must have the more-or-less constant wrestling with the words that express difficult ideas and moving targets. I find the shape-shifting of words and their meanings fascinating; this is the sociologist in me. However, I hope we can agree to (forgive the cliché) "keep the big things big." The Jim Crow Museum was founded on the idea that objects of racial intolerance could be used to teach about race, race relations, and racism—and that those lessons, shared through painfully honest dialogues, would result in less racism. We can call this a pursuit of tolerance, appreciation, respect, acceptance, inclusion, or justice. Those are all good pursuits.

I will end with a story. One of my daughters plays on an elite soccer team, which means her practices are never done on time. One day I sat in the van with my other daughter waiting for practice to end. Nearby several white boys were clowning in front of two girls. They were all teenagers. One of the boys wore a blackfaced mask and he mocked the mannerisms of "street blacks." He turned toward us and I immediately looked at my daughter. She had lowered her head and covered her face. If you have a child then you know what I felt. If your skin is dark then you know why I do what I do.

CHAPTER TWO

An Unorthodox Teaching Tool

Professor O.C. Nix was born too soon, and he did not like it. A similar mind—keenly analytical, grasping the nuances of macro- and micro-level historical patterns—would today be employed at one of the nation's flagship institutions. But he is dead and most of his life was lived during and under Jim Crow segregation. He attended segregated schools and learned firsthand that "separate but equal" was a misnomer; no, it was a smirk-in-your-face lie. He searched for books and read every one he found. He wanted to know what the brightest minds knew. He read all the so-called Great Books, read them and read them again. He took notes, argued with the white writers, though they were dead, and even if they were alive would not have thought him worthy of a conversation. He traveled when he could, which was not often because he was for many years poor. He earned a college degree and then advanced degrees all the while struggling with and against the taken-for-granted beliefs that black skin and rural poverty were markers of inferiority and ignorance.

He was a history professor at Jarvis Christian College. He was black and all the students were black. It was confusing when I sat in his course several decades ago, but now I understand how a man, a proud man, a hurt man, could come into the classroom one day and be encouraging. "Do not let anyone, any book, any movie, any wayward glance, convince you that you are not smart"—and on the very next day spit self- and group-hatred venom. "You are lazy and this is why the white man keeps you down." It made us angry. It made us study. This is what living under Jim Crow did to some minds, some social selves—it stained them, warped them, took good people and broke them.

One day, Professor Nix came into the classroom with a chauffeur's cap. He set the hat down and asked us to explain its historical significance to Jim Crow. Hands went up. The obvious answer was that Jim Crow era black men were denied most economic opportunities, and chauffeuring was one of the few jobs open to them. He said that answer was wrong, too shallow. "Use your heads, think, students." Someone else said that chauffeurs and butlers were jobs that placed blacks in contact with whites and thus afforded black men, in rare cases, opportunities to learn more about the "larger society." No, that was wrong.

He talked about being poor, too poor to own shoes, too poor to do more than hope—said that we could never understand that type of poverty. And, then, he started talking about walking—walking until your feet hurt. It was a soft rant, but a rant nevertheless, about walking everywhere, walking under the hot southern sun, walking and dreaming of a day when even a poor black man would own a brand-new shiny car. This was, he said, a silly dream for almost all rural blacks in the 1940s and 1950s. A new car, a pretty car, was a white man's privilege, and not just any white man, a white man with money.

Then he talked about the emergence of a professional class of blacks—mostly preachers, doctors, morticians, and college professors. Although they lived before the victories of the civil rights movement they had found a piece of the American Dream. They benefited from racial segregation—black people had to use their services. Their wealth was modest by comparison to their white peers but substantial when compared to most black people. This "Black Bourgeoisie"¹ wanted the material evidence of success: nice homes, stylish clothing, and new cars, and they bought these things; thereby achieving the trappings of the white, bourgeois ideal.

But, they had to be careful. Though they idealized the bourgeois (read: white) ideal—and at least partially achieved it—there were times and places when they could not escape their blackness. For example, a drive through the South, especially through small towns, brought the possibility of being stopped by a white police officer, or maybe being forced to get gasoline from a white attendant. In either case the white person might be angered by a black person owning a car. A black man owning a car, especially a nice looking car, would have, in some communities, violated Jim Crow etiquette, and the punishment might have been severe. Professor Nix put the chauffeur's cap on his head and said, "Wearing this cap saved lives."

The day remains vivid in my mind. Years later, at the Ohio State University I was introduced to the sociological theory called symbolic interactionism. One of the premises of that theory is that no object has any inherent meaning. We give meanings to objects and we do it as we interact with others. Obviously, a cap is not inherently racist, nor does

it have a meaning that is inherently linked to racism. But we know, individually and collectively, that the chauffeur's cap's meanings are associated with a particular job and with a social status—and with particular racial groups. Objects don't have intrinsic meanings but they do have *real* meanings. Wearing the chauffeur's cap was a shorthand way of saying, *I am a servant, a driver of others. This car does not belong to me. It is too expensive for me, too good for me, too good for people like me. I am not a threat to you or the social order. I know my place.*

The anecdote about the chauffeur's cap planted a seed in my mind. I never forgot the story and I never stopped thinking of ways to use objects to teach about race, race relations, and racism, and this includes objects that do not appear to have any racial significance.

It took me a long time to learn how to teach and an even longer time to learn how to teach with racist objects. One person who helped me was Dr. Tamsey Andrews, who worked at Ferris State University as the grants director shortly before she died in 2002. Dr. Andrews, who received a PhD in classical archaeology from Brandeis and a master of education from Harvard, argued that the objects in the museum should be treated as value-neutral art. Her argument troubled me on several levels. First, like

The museum expanded and reopened in April 2012.

The museum draws people from all walks, including Henry Rollins, host of *10 Things You Don't Know About*, and Professor Henry Louis Gates Jr., the famed historian.

many novices, I saw art as something aesthetically pleasant, intellectually provocative, or in some other way laudable. The racist objects in the museum seemed, to me, the antithesis of art. Second, how could a racist object (think of a postcard with a black man being hanged or beaten) be value-neutral? There was, after all, a message being sent to the viewer of the postcard, especially if that viewer was an African American living under Jim Crow segregation. Finally, there was the implication with her approach that no interpretation was more valid than any other, and if I believed that then I would have to accept that an interpretation derived from a racist, oppressive worldview was as valid as one opposed to that interpretation.

I shared these concerns with Dr. Andrews and she suggested that I read about Visual Thinking Strategies, a pedagogical tool used in museums and schools. At the risk of being too simplistic, Visual Thinking Strategies are used in small groups where a museum docent (or a teacher) facilitates a discussion by asking general, nonthreatening questions that lead the students toward greater understanding, of both themselves and the art. You might begin by directing students to look at a print by Paul Klee, the Swiss expressionist painter. You start with, "What's going on

in this painting?" Students are allowed to answer any way they deem relevant. After each student's response, you paraphrase what they said. This lets students know that you understand them and helps ensure that everyone in the class has heard the comments. Repeating what students say also helps them realize that their contributions to discussions are valid. You might next ask, "What do you see that makes you say that?" After they respond, you probe with, "What more can you find?"

Americans are reluctant to talk about race relations in settings where their ideas may be challenged, and there are many reasons for that reluctance: a lack of confidence in one's communication skills and not wanting to say one thing while meaning another; a fear of saying something that sounds racially insensitive or racist; the dread of getting angry or sounding angry; the sincere conviction that nothing good can come from discussing race relations and racism because these are "old" conversations; the trepidation of experiencing an argument, and so forth. No pedagogical tool, including Visual Thinking Strategies, can make people talk about race relations, but this approach does help create a safe, nonthreatening space where honest, facilitated discussions are possible—and, truth be told, that was hard for me when I first used the approach.

Visitors viewing the section that deals with black people as targets.

Yes, I wanted the Jim Crow Museum to be a place where people talked openly and honestly about race relations; I wanted the museum to be a "safe" place, but equally important, I wanted the museum to be a place where ideas and beliefs were challenged. In other words, I wanted the museum to be safe but uncomfortable. It is obvious to me now that I was struggling with two roles: facilitator and activist. The facilitator role fit neatly into the Visual Thinking Strategies, but the activist wanted to advocate, correct, proselytize, and tell students/visitors what to think. I would hold an object—say, matches with a grotesquely caricatured black child—and ask, "What do you see?" Often, someone would say, simply and succinctly, "A child," or worse, "A cute little boy." The activist in me wanted to scream, "What do you mean, you only see a child?" or "Are you serious, you actually believe this child is cute?" I wanted to stop the dialogue and begin a monologue about the role that racial caricatures played in supporting the Jim Crow racial hierarchy. I wanted to passionately detail the ways that African American children had been depicted as naked or near-naked, physically ugly, poor, illiterate "baby coons." I wanted to make sure that all the visitors understood the psychological harm done to children of color in this country—and I wanted to do all of this as soon as I heard "A cute little boy."

If you do something a long time, you should get better at it. There are two premises that I accept today that I did not accept years ago: you have to reach people where they are; and, intellectually beating down someone makes teaching them improbable. It is unproductive to criticize someone because they do not know who Jim Crow was or what Jim Crow laws were,

Hateful Things is a traveling exhibition that uses objects from the museum.

or because they believe that Aunt Jemima and Uncle Ben honor black people and the Klan is misunderstood, or because after looking at a caricatured image of an African American child they announce that the child is cute. I have gotten better at allowing others to speak openly (even when what they say disappoints me) and have gotten better at allowing others to "save face." In these ways, Visual Thinking Strategies has helped me be a better facilitator. It is a good way to start. I am still learning to trust the process and still learning to trust the abilities and willingness of people to learn about race relations. But I still believe, and may always believe, that a place where you are safe to express your views does not mean that those views cannot and should not be challenged. The facilitator knows something that the activist may not: the teacher does not always have to be one that challenges; sometimes the other students will challenge, and sometimes, people will challenge themselves.

I will never believe that the racist objects in the Jim Crow Museum are value-neutral art or value-neutral objects. I understand that no object has intrinsic meaning but it would be naive of me to believe that the 1921 "Nigger Milk" cartoon of a black child drinking ink is value-neutral. The many objects that defamed African Americans both reflected and shaped values. The objects in the museum are, in a real way, propaganda. I do believe that propaganda can be explored, examined, critiqued, and understood. This brings me again to Visual Thinking Strategies: it is not necessary for me to accept all of its underlying assumptions. This approach works for me because I have modified it. I begin by asking visitors and students to examine objects carefully. Then I ask, "What do you see?" "What else do you see?" "What does this mean to you?" I give them a loose rein. I try to communicate that they are free to express any and all ideas, values, tastes, and beliefs. Next, I probe. "Why do you believe that?" "What makes you say that?" "Where do you think that value came from?" Again, I try to facilitate the discussion without dominating it (that's hard for me). More questions. "What does this image remind you of?" "Can you see how someone would view this differently?" At that point I usually "burst" and start lecturing.

CHAPTER THREE

Understanding Jim Crow

For some people, especially those who came of age after landmark civil rights legislation was passed, it is difficult to understand what it was like to be an African American living under Jim Crow segregation. Most of the young people who visit the Jim Crow Museum have little or no knowledge about restrictive covenants, literacy tests, poll taxes, lynchings, and other oppressive features of the Jim Crow racial hierarchy. Even those students who have some familiarity with the Jim Crow period initially view the museum's holdings as relics of a distant, irrelevant past—until it is revealed how much of this racially charged material is produced today. A proper understanding of race relations in this country must include a solid knowledge of Jim Crow—how it emerged, what it was like, and how it ended.

> "Come listen all you galls and boys,
> I's just from Tucky-hoe
> I'm going to sing a little song,
> My name is Jim Crow.
> Weel about and turn about and do jis so,
> Eb'ry time I weel about I jump Jim Crow."

These words are from the song, "Jim Crow," as it appeared in sheet music written by Thomas Dartmouth "Daddy" Rice. Rice, a struggling actor (he did short solo skits between play scenes) at the Park Theater in New York, happened upon a black person singing the above song. Some accounts say it was an old black slave who walked with difficulty, others say it was a ragged black stable boy. Whether modeled on an old

MR BERT A. WILLIAMS
AS "A FAIRY QUEEN"
"WON'T YOU COME AND DANCE WITH ME"

man or a young boy we will never know, but we know that in 1828 Rice appeared on stage as Jim Crow—an exaggerated, highly stereotypical black character.

Rice, a white actor, was one of the early American performers to wear blackface makeup—his face darkened with burnt cork. His Jim Crow song-and-dance routine was an astounding success that took him from Louisville to Cincinnati to Pittsburgh to Philadelphia and finally to New York in 1832. He also performed to great acclaim in London and Dublin. By then Jim Crow was a stock character in minstrel shows, along with counterparts Jim Dandy and Zip Coon. Rice's subsequent blackface characters were Sambos, coons, and dandies. White audiences were receptive to the portrayals of blacks as singing, dancing, grinning buffoons.

The minstrel show was one of the first native forms of American entertainment, and Rice was rightly regarded as the Father of American minstrelsy.[1] He had many imitators. In 1843, four white men from New York, billed as the Virginia Minstrels, darkened their faces and imitated the singing and dancing of blacks. They used violins, castanets, banjos, bones, and tambourines. Their routine was successful and they were invited to tour the country. In 1845, the Christy Minstrels originated many features of the minstrel show, including the seating of the blackface performers in a semicircle on stage, with the tambourine player (Mr. Tambo) at one end, and the bones player (Mr. Bones) at the other; the singing of songs, called Ethiopian melodies, with harmonized choruses; and the humorous banter of jokes between the endmen and the performer in the middle seat (Mr. Interlocutor). These performers were sometimes called Ethiopian Delineators and the shows were popularly referred to as "coon shows."

Rice and his imitators, by their stereotypical depictions of blacks, helped to popularize the belief that blacks were lazy, stupid, inherently less human, and unworthy of integration. During the years that blacks were being victimized by lynch mobs, they were also victimized by the racist caricatures propagated through novels, sheet music, theatrical plays, and minstrel shows. Ironically, years later when blacks replaced white minstrels, the blacks also blackened their faces, thereby pretending to be whites pretending

LEFT: This 1904 postcard is from the Raphael Tuck & Sons series "Coon Studies." **BELOW:** Made in 1850, this plate from England is one of the oldest pieces in the museum.

Bob man. Wash i mantil. 1941

Evelyn Schultz

1971

to be blacks. They too performed the coon shows which dehumanized blacks and helped establish the desirability of racial segregation.

Daddy Rice, the original Jim Crow, became rich and famous because of his skills as a minstrel. He lived an extravagant lifestyle, but when he died in New York on September 19, 1860, he was in poverty. The minstrel shows were popular between 1850 and 1870, but they lost much of their national popularity with the coming of motion pictures and radio. Unfortunately for blacks, the minstrel shows continued in small towns, and caricatured portrayals of blacks found greater expression in motion pictures and on radio shows.

By 1838, the term *Jim Crow* was used as a collective racial epithet for blacks, not as offensive as *nigger*, but similar to *coon* or *darkie*. The popularity of minstrel shows clearly aided the spread of Jim Crow as a racial slur. This use of the term only lasted half a century. By the end of the nineteenth century, the words Jim Crow were less likely to be used to derisively describe blacks; instead, the phrase Jim Crow was a synonym for the racial caste system which operated primarily, but not exclusively, in southern and border states between 1877 and the mid-1960s.

LEFT: Pictures of a small-town minstrel show, 1947. **ABOVE:** In the early 1900s, the M. Stein Cosmetic Company of New York was one of the nation's leading manufacturers of theatrical makeup and greasepaints.

Jim Crow was more than a series of rigid antiblack laws. It was a way of life. Under Jim Crow, African Americans were relegated to the status of second-class citizens. Jim Crow represented the legitimization of antiblack racism. Many Christian ministers and theologians taught that whites were the chosen people, blacks were cursed to be servants, and God supported racial segregation. Craniologists, eugenicists, phrenologists, and Social Darwinists at every educational level buttressed the belief that blacks were innately intellectually and culturally inferior to whites. Pro-segregation politicians gave eloquent speeches on the great danger of integration: the mongrelization of the white race. Newspaper and magazine writers routinely referred to blacks as niggers, coons, and darkies; and worse, their articles reinforced antiblack stereotypes. Even children's games portrayed blacks as inferior beings. All major societal institutions reflected and supported the oppression of blacks.

The Jim Crow system was undergirded by the following beliefs or rationalizations: whites were superior to blacks in all important ways, including but not limited to intelligence, morality, and civilized behavior; sexual relations between blacks and whites would produce a mongrel

LEFT: This minstrel joke book was published in 1916 by Wehman Bros., in New York.
ABOVE: As recent as the 1960s, blackface minstrel shows were performed in churches, convention centers, high schools, and on college campuses.

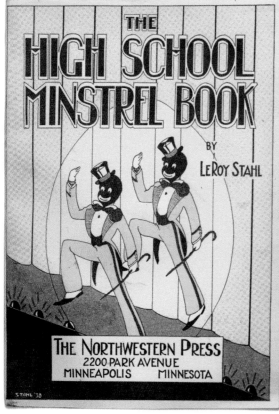

DELRAY BEACH TAXI

Telephone: CRestwood 6-6464

72 S. E. 4th Ave. — Catering to the White Clientele

ACME TAXI

Telephone: CRestwood 8-1388

24 HOUR SERVICE

race which would destroy the United States; treating blacks as equals would encourage interracial sexual unions; any activity which suggested social equality encouraged interracial sexual relations; if necessary, violence must be used to keep blacks at the bottom of the racial hierarchy. The following Jim Crow etiquette norms show how inclusive and pervasive these beliefs were:

a) A black male could not offer to shake hands with a white male because it implied being socially equal. Obviously, a black male could not offer his hand or any other part of his body to a white woman, because he risked being accused of rape.

b) Blacks and whites were not supposed to eat together. If they did eat together, whites were to be served first, and some sort of partition was to be placed between them.

c) Under no circumstance was a black male to offer to light the cigarette of a white female—that gesture implied intimacy.

d) Blacks were not allowed to show public affection toward one another in public, especially kissing, because it offended whites.

e) Jim Crow etiquette prescribed that blacks were introduced to whites, never whites to blacks. For example: "Mr. Peters (the white person), this is Charlie (the black person), who I spoke to you about."

f) Whites did not use courtesy titles of respect when referring to blacks, for example, Mr., Mrs., Miss., Sir, or Ma'am. Instead, blacks were called by their first names. Blacks had to use courtesy titles when referring to whites, and were not allowed to call them by their first names.

LEFT: The pervasiveness of Jim Crow attitudes is evident in this postcard (postmarked 1905), minstrel book, 1938, and movie poster from the 1950s.
ABOVE: Business card (circa 1940s).

STATE OF LOUISIANA
PARISH OF CADDO

1930

No 3880   Shreveport, La. 12-30 1930.

Received of Mrs Josie L Adams

of Ward No. 9, Caddo Parish, Louisiana.

One Dollar for Poll Tax for the Year 1930.

T. R. HUGHES, Tax Collector

$1.00   { WHITE } { COLORED }   By J R P Allison

Deputy.

EXCLUSIVE

WHITE LABORERS
TRACK WORK
OHIO

NICKEL PLATE ROAD   NICKEL PLATE ROAD

Colored School Report Card
CLARKSVILLE, TENN.

REPORT OF Hester, George M 1929-1930.

SUBJECTS	SECOND TERM						
	Feb. 21	Mar.21	Apr.18	May23	Av.	Exam.	FINAL GRADE
Reading	95	95	95	95			95
Writing	90	85	80	80			84
Spelling	95	90	95	95			94
Arithmetic	90	88	90	95			91
English							
Geography							
History							
Hygiene				Honor Roll			
Music							
Drawing							
Effort	8	8	8	8			8
Deportment	8	8	8	8			8
Days Present	25	20	20	24			89
Days Absent	0	0	0	1			1
Times Tardy			1				1
Special Notice			Promoted				

See other side.   General Average 91

L. Williams Teacher.   H. L. ALLISON, Principal.

ORIG.
1928
POLL TAX RECEIPT
STATE OF TEXAS
COUNTY OF
ZAPATA

R. P. L.

NO. 91

DATE 1/30 19 29

RECEIVED OF Erna R. Shoelt

PRECINCT	ADDRESS Zapata						R. F. D.	BOX
1	AGE	LENGTH OF RESIDENCE			SEX	MALE	OCCUPATION	
WARD		STATE	COUNTY	CITY		FEMALE		
	25	25	2	2	RACE	WHITE / COLORED	School Teacher	

THE SUM OF ONE AND 75/100 DOLLARS IN PAYMENT OF POLL TAX FOR THE YEAR SHOWN ABOVE, THE SAID TAXPAYER BEING DULY SWORN BY ME SAYS THAT THE ABOVE IS CORRECT, ALL OF WHICH I CERTIFY

BY _____   DEPUTY _____

Ignacio Sanchez

TAX COLLECTOR OF ABOVE SAID COUNTY

g) If a black person rode in a car driven by a white person, the black person sat in the back seat or in the back of a truck.

h) White motorists had the right-of-way at all intersections.

Stetson Kennedy, the author of *Jim Crow Guide*, offered these general rules that blacks were supposed to observe in conversing with whites:

1) Never assert or even intimate that a white person is lying.
2) Never impute dishonorable intentions to a white person.
3) Never suggest that a white person is from an inferior class.
4) Never lay claim to, or overtly demonstrate, superior knowledge or intelligence.
5) Never curse a white person.
6) Never laugh derisively at a white person.
7) Never comment upon the appearance of a white female.[2]

Jim Crow etiquette operated in conjunction with Jim Crow laws. When most people think of Jim Crow they think of laws (not the Jim Crow etiquette) which excluded blacks from public transportation and facilities, juries, jobs, and neighborhoods. The passage of the Thirteenth, Fourteenth, and Fifteenth Amendments to the United States Constitution granted blacks the same legal protections as whites. But after 1877, with the election of Rutherford B. Hayes, southern and border states began restricting the liberties of blacks. Unfortunately for blacks, the Supreme Court helped undermine the Constitutional protections of blacks with the infamous *Plessy v. Ferguson* (1896) case, which legitimized Jim Crow laws and the Jim Crow way of life.

In 1890, Louisiana passed the "Separate Car Law," which purported to aid passenger comfort by creating "equal but separate" cars for blacks and whites. This was a ruse. No public accommodations, including railway travel, provided blacks with equal facilities. The law made it illegal for blacks to sit in coach seats reserved for whites, and whites could not sit in seats reserved for blacks. In 1891, a group of blacks decided to test the Jim Crow law. They had Homer A. Plessy, who was seven-eighths white and one-eighth black (therefore, black), sit in the

LEFT: During the Jim Crow period, racial segregation permeated every part of American society as evidenced by these objects from the 1920s and 1930s. ABOVE: In the 1940s, Anderson County, South Carolina, was the home of one of the nation's largest fairs for African Americans. **47**

whites-only railroad coach. He was arrested. Plessy's lawyer argued that Louisiana did not have the right to label one citizen as white and another black for the purposes of restricting their rights and privileges. In *Plessy*, the Supreme Court stated that so long as state governments provided legal process and legal freedoms for blacks, equal to those of whites, they could maintain separate institutions to facilitate these rights. The High Court, by a 7–2 vote, upheld the Louisiana law, declaring that racial separation did not necessarily mean an abrogation of equality. In practice, *Plessy* represented the legitimization of two societies: one white and advantaged; the other black, disadvantaged, and despised. Stated differently, it made the racial hierarchy—with whites on the top and blacks on the bottom—legal.

Blacks were denied the right to vote by grandfather clauses (laws that restricted the right to vote to people whose ancestors had voted before the Civil War), poll taxes (fees charged to poor people), white primaries (only Democrats could vote, only whites could be Democrats), and literacy tests ("Name all the Vice Presidents and Supreme Court Justices throughout America's history"). *Plessy* sent the message to southern and border states that discrimination against blacks was acceptable.

Jim Crow states passed statutes severely regulating social interactions between the races. Jim Crow signs were placed above water fountains, door entrances and exits, and in front of public facilities. There were separate hospitals for blacks and whites, separate prisons, separate public and private schools, separate churches, separate cemeteries, separate public restrooms, and separate public accommodations. In most instances, the black facilities were grossly inferior—generally older, less well-kept. In other cases, there were no black facilities—no colored public restroom, no public beach, no place to sit or eat. *Plessy* gave Jim Crow states a legal way to ignore their constitutional obligations to their black citizens.

Jim Crow laws touched every aspect of everyday life. For example, in 1935, Oklahoma prohibited blacks and whites from boating together. Boating implied social equality. In 1905, Georgia established separate parks for blacks and whites. In 1930, Birmingham, Alabama, made it illegal for blacks and whites to play checkers or dominoes together. Here are some typical Jim Crow laws, as compiled by the Martin Luther King Jr. National Historic Site Interpretive Staff:

- *Barbers.* No colored barber shall serve as a barber (to) white girls or women (Georgia).
- *Blind Wards.* The board of trustees shall . . . maintain a separate building . . . on separate ground for the admission, care,

This postcard was a part of the Bamforth Comic series "Black Kids," made in London, circa 1907–1915.

" I'm afraid of the dark ! "

instruction, and support of all blind persons of the colored or black race (Louisiana).

- *Burial.* The officer in charge shall not bury, or allow to be buried, any colored persons upon ground set apart or used for the burial of white persons (Georgia).
- *Buses.* All passenger stations in this state operated by any motor transportation company shall have separate waiting rooms or space and separate ticket windows for the white and colored races (Alabama).
- *Child Custody.* It shall be unlawful for any parent, relative, or other white person in this State, having the control or custody of any white child, by right of guardianship, natural or acquired, or otherwise, to dispose of, give or surrender such white child permanently into the custody, control, maintenance, or support, of a negro (South Carolina).
- *Education.* The schools for white children and the schools for negro children shall be conducted separately (Florida).
- *Libraries.* The state librarian is directed to fit up and maintain a separate place for the use of the colored people who may come

LEFT: Jim Crow Jubilee sheet music, 1847.
RIGHT: Postcard, postmarked 1911.

A Clear Case of Suicide

to the library for the purpose of reading books or periodicals (North Carolina).

- *Mental Hospitals.* The Board of Control shall see that proper and distinct apartments are arranged for said patients, so that in no case shall Negroes and white persons be together (Georgia).
- *Militia.* The white and colored militia shall be separately enrolled, and shall never be compelled to serve in the same organization. No organization of colored troops shall be permitted where white troops are available, and while permitted to be organized, colored troops shall be under command of white officers (North Carolina).
- *Nurses.* No person or corporation shall require any white female nurse to nurse in wards or rooms in hospitals, either public or private, in which negro men are placed (Alabama).
- *Prisons.* The warden shall see that the white convicts shall have separate apartments for both eating and sleeping from the negro convicts (Mississippi).
- *Reform Schools.* The children of white and colored races committed to the houses of reform shall be kept entirely separate from each other (Kentucky).
- *Teaching.* Any instructor who shall teach in any school, college or institution where members of the white and colored race are received and enrolled as pupils for instruction shall be deemed

This 1890s card is a popular culture expression of the nineteenth-century theories that claimed that "negroes will die out."

THIS SPACE FOR WRITING MESSAGES.
10,–30,–24,

We reached
Aunt Libbie
7 O'clock, had
a lovely ride.
This picture
showes what they
do to the bad
people of Del.
Aunt Harriet

POST CARD

THIS SPACE FOR ADDRESS

Master Edwin S.
Goshen
R.F.D.   N.Y.
M. Stephen Smith

THE WHIPPING POST, DOVER, DEL.

guilty of a misdemeanor, and upon conviction thereof, shall be fined . . . (Oklahoma).

- *Wine and Beer.* All persons licensed to conduct the business of selling beer or wine . . . shall serve either white people exclusively or colored people exclusively and shall not sell to the two races within the same room at any time (Georgia).[3]

The Jim Crow laws and system of etiquette were supported by violence, real and threatened. Blacks who violated Jim Crow norms, for example, drinking from the white water fountain or trying to vote, risked their homes, their jobs, even their lives. Whites could physically beat blacks with impunity. Blacks had little legal recourse against these assaults because the Jim Crow criminal justice system was all-white: police, prosecutors, judges, juries, and prison officials. Violence was instrumental for Jim Crow. It was a method of social control. The most extreme forms of Jim Crow violence were lynchings.

Lynchings were public, often sadistic, murders carried out by mobs. Between 1882, when the first reliable data were collected, and 1968, when lynchings had become rare, there were 4,730 known lynchings, including 3,440 black men and women. Most of the victims of lynch law were hanged or shot, but some were burned at the stake, castrated, beaten with clubs, or dismembered. In the mid-1800s, whites constituted the majority of victims (and perpetrators), but by the period of Radical Reconstruction, blacks became the most frequent lynching victims. This is an early indication that lynching was used as an intimidation tool to keep blacks, in this case the newly freed people, "in their places." The great majority of lynchings occurred in southern and border states, where the resentment against blacks ran deepest. According to the social economist Gunnar Myrdal, "The southern states account for nine-tenths of the lynchings. More than two-thirds of the remaining one-tenth occurred in the six states which immediately border the South."[4]

Many whites claimed that although lynchings were distasteful, they were necessary supplements to the criminal justice system because blacks were prone to violent crimes, especially the rape of white women. Under Jim Crow any and all sexual interactions between black men and white women was illegal, illicit, socially repugnant, and within the Jim Crow definition of rape. Although only 19.2 percent of the lynching victims between 1882 to 1951 were even accused of rape, lynch law was often supported on the popular belief that lynchings were necessary to protect white women from black rapists. Myrdal refutes this belief in this way: "There is much reason to believe that this figure [19.2 percent] has been inflated by the fact that a mob which makes the accusation of rape is

TOP: Caption on back reads, "Florida – Early 1900s: Negroes Rounded up and shot."
BOTTOM: Message on back, "This picture shows what they do to the bad people of Del."

53

secure from any further investigation; by the broad Southern definition of rape to include all sexual relations between Negro men and white women; and by the psychopathic fears of white women in their contacts with Negro men."[5] Most blacks were lynched for demanding civil rights, violating Jim Crow etiquette or laws, or in the aftermath of race riots.

Lynchings were most common in small and middle-sized towns where blacks often were economic competitors to the local whites. These whites resented any economic and political gains made by blacks. Lynchers were seldom arrested, and if arrested, rarely convicted. Sociologist Arthur Raper estimated that "at least one-half of the lynchings are carried out with police officers participating, and that in nine-tenths of the others the officers either condone or wink at the mob action."[6] Lynching served many purposes: it was cheap entertainment; it served as a rallying, uniting point for whites; it functioned as an ego-massage for low-income, low-status whites; it was a method of defending white domination and helped stop or slow down the fledgling social equality movement.

Lynch mobs directed their hatred against one (sometimes several) victims. The victim was an example of what happened to a black man who tried to vote, who looked at a white woman, or who tried to get a white man's job. Unfortunately for blacks, sometimes the mob was not satisfied to murder a single or several victims. Instead, in the spirit of pogroms, the mobs went into black communities and destroyed additional lives and property. Their immediate goal was to drive out—through death or expulsion—all blacks; the larger goal was to maintain, at all costs, white supremacy. These pogrom-like actions are often referred to as riots, yet Gunnar Myrdal was right when he described these "riots" as "a terrorization or massacre . . . a mass lynching."[7] Interestingly, these mass lynchings were primarily urban phenomena, whereas the lynching of single victims was primarily a rural phenomenon.

James Weldon Johnson, the famous black writer, labeled 1919 as "The Red Summer." It was red from racial tension; it was red from blood-letting. During the summer of 1919, there were race riots in Chicago, Illinois; Knoxville and Nashville, Tennessee; Charleston, South Carolina; Omaha, Nebraska; and two dozen other cities. W.E.B. Du Bois, the black social scientist and civil rights activist, wrote: "During that year seventy-seven Negroes were lynched, of whom one was a woman and eleven were soldiers; of these, fourteen were publicly burned, eleven of them being burned alive. That year there were race riots large and small in twenty-six American cities including thirty-eight killed in a Chicago riot of August; from twenty-five to fifty in Phillips County, Arkansas; and six killed in Washington."[8]

There is no identifying data on this picture.

The riots of 1919 were not the first or last mass lynchings of blacks, as evidenced by the race riots in Wilmington, North Carolina (1898); Atlanta, Georgia (1906); Springfield, Illinois (1908); East St. Louis, Illinois (1917); Tulsa, Oklahoma (1921); and Detroit, Michigan (1943). Joseph Boskin found that the riots of the 1900s had the following traits:

1) In each of the race riots, with few exceptions, it was white people that sparked the incident by attacking black people.
2) In the majority of the riots, some extraordinary social condition prevailed at the time of the riot: prewar social changes, wartime mobility, postwar adjustment, or economic depression.
3) The majority of the riots occurred during the hot summer months.
4) Rumor played an extremely important role in causing many riots. Rumors of some criminal activity by blacks against whites perpetuated the actions of the white mobs.
5) The police force, more than any other institution, was invariably involved as a precipitating cause or perpetuating factor in the riots. In almost every one of the riots, the police sided with the attackers, either by actually participating or by failing to quell the attack.
6) In almost every instance, the fighting occurred within the black community.[9]

Boskin omitted the following: the mass media, especially newspapers, often published inflammatory articles about black criminal suspects immediately before the riots; blacks were not only killed, but their homes and businesses were looted, and many who did not flee were left homeless; and, the goal of the white rioters, as was true of white lynchers of single victims, was to instill fear and terror into blacks, thereby buttressing white domination. The Jim Crow hierarchy could not work without violence being used against those on the bottom rung. Historian George Fredrickson stated it this way: "Lynching represented . . . a way of using fear and terror to check 'dangerous' tendencies in a black community considered to be ineffectively regimented or supervised. As such it constituted a confession that the regular institutions of a segregated society provided an inadequate measure of day-to-day control."[10] Many blacks resisted the indignities of Jim Crow and, far too often, they paid for their bravery with their lives.

The Jim Crow Museum has a small section that houses artifacts related to the civil rights movement. There is a picture of Nettie Hunt and her daughter, Nickie, sitting on steps of the Supreme Court Building on May 18, 1954, the day following the High Court's historic decision in

In 1900, Charles Carroll wrote *The Negro a Beast; or, In the Image of God.* Carroll claimed that white people were made in the image and likeness of God and that Adam gave birth to the white race only, while Negroes were soulless, immoral, ugly pre-Adamite beasts. According to Carroll, race mixing spoiled God's racial plan of creation.

57

NOTICE!

STOP

Help Save The Youth of America

DON'T BUY NEGRO RECORDS

(If you don't want to serve negroes in your place of business, then do not have negro records on your juke box or listen to negro records on the radio.)

The screaming, idiotic words, and savage music of these records are undermining the morals of our white youth in America.

Call the advertisers of the radio stations that play this type of music and complain to them!

Don't Let Your Children Buy, or Listen

To These Negro Records

For additional copies of this circular, write
CITIZENS' COUNCIL OF GREATER NEW ORLEANS, INC.
509 Delta Building   New Orleans Louisiana 70112

Brown v. Board of Education. The mother, smiling at her daughter, holds a newspaper with the headline "High Court Bans Segregation in Public Schools." The museum has photographs of arrested Freedom Riders, young activists who rode interstate buses into the segregated south. One of their buses was fire-bombed. Some of them were beaten by white mobs. The Jim Crow Museum has a reproduction of one of the signs used at the 1963 March on Washington. The sign reads, "I AM A MAN." But my favorite object in the section—maybe my favorite piece in the entire museum—is one of the ink pens that President Lyndon B. Johnson used to sign the Civil Rights Act of 1964, the most comprehensive and important civil rights legislation of the twentieth century. This act outlawed discrimination against racial, ethnic, national and religious minorities, and women. It ended racial segregation in schools, workplaces, and public accommodations. In other words, the Civil Rights Act ended de jure (legal) Jim Crow.

LEFT: This 1950s flyer was distributed by the Citizen's Council of Greater New Orleans, one of many white supremacist groups that were founded primarily to oppose racial integration. **ABOVE:** This 1960s license plate mocked two of that decade's slogans: "The New Negro" and "The New Democrat"—by portraying Martin Luther King Jr. and Lyndon B. Johnson as rats.

CHAPTER FOUR

A Caricatured Family

Violence, real and threatened, was a major underpinning of the Jim Crow racial caste system that operated in parts of the United States from the 1870s to the 1960s. The racial hierarchy was also supported by millions of everyday objects that caricatured and stereotyped African Americans. Some of the caricatures were created as defenses for slavery but their utility extended into the Jim Crow period. This chapter looks at three major caricatures of African Americans: the mammy, the Tom, and the picaninny.

Real Mammies

From slavery through the Jim Crow era, the mammy image served the political, social, and economic interests of mainstream white America. During slavery, the mammy caricature was posited as proof that blacks—in this case, black women—were contented, even happy, as slaves. Her wide grin, hearty laugher, and loyal servitude were offered as evidence of the supposed humanity of the institution of slavery.

This was the mammy caricature, and, like all caricatures, it contained a little truth surrounded by a larger lie. The caricature portrayed an obese, coarse, maternal figure. She had great love for her white "family," but often treated her own family with disdain. Although she had children, sometimes many, she was completely desexualized. She "belonged" to the white family, though it was rarely stated. She was a faithful worker. She typically had no black friends; the white family was her entire world. Obviously, the mammy caricature was more myth than accurate portrayal.

Catherine Clinton, a historian, claimed that real antebellum mammies were rare:

> Records do acknowledge the presence of female slaves who served as the "right hand" of plantation mistresses. Yet documents from the planter class during the first fifty years following the American Revolution reveal only a handful of such examples. Not until after Emancipation did black women run white households or occupy in any significant number the special positions ascribed to them in folklore and fiction. The Mammy was created by white Southerners to redeem the relationship between black women and white men within slave society in response to the antislavery attack from the North during the ante-bellum period. In the primary records from before the Civil War, hard evidence for its existence simply does not appear.[1]

According to Patricia Turner, professor of African American and African Studies, before the Civil War only very wealthy whites could afford the luxury of "utilizing the (black) women as house servants rather than as field hands."[2] Moreover, Turner claims that house servants were usually mixed-race, skinny (blacks were not given much food), and young (fewer than 10 percent of black women lived beyond fifty years). Why were the fictional mammies so different from their real-life counterparts? The answer lies squarely within the complex sexual relations between blacks and whites.

Abolitionists argued that one of the many brutal aspects of slavery was that slave owners sexually exploited their female slaves, especially light-skinned ones who approximated the mainstream definition of female sexual attractiveness. The mammy caricature was deliberately constructed to suggest ugliness. Mammy was portrayed as dark-skinned, often pitch black, in a society that regarded black skin as ugly, tainted. She was obese, sometimes morbidly overweight. Moreover, she was often portrayed as old, or at least middle-aged. The attempt was to desexualize Mammy. The implicit assumption was this: No reasonable white man would choose a fat, elderly black woman instead of the idealized white woman. The black mammy was portrayed as lacking all sexual and sensual qualities. The de-eroticizing of Mammy meant that the white wife—and by extension, the white family—was safe.

The sexual exploitation of black women by white men was common during the antebellum period, and this was true irrespective of the economic relationship involved. In other words, black women were sexually exploited by rich whites, middle-class whites, and poor whites. Sexual relations between blacks and whites—whether consensual or rape—were

The portrayal of black women as nurturers is apparent on a postcard postmarked 1905, another postcard postmarked 1910, and a 1920s photograph.

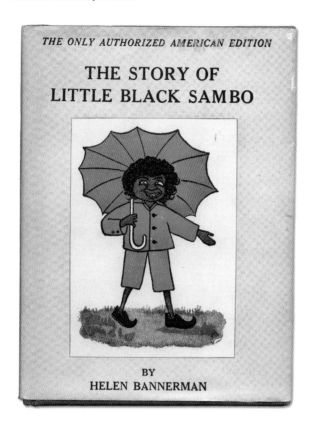

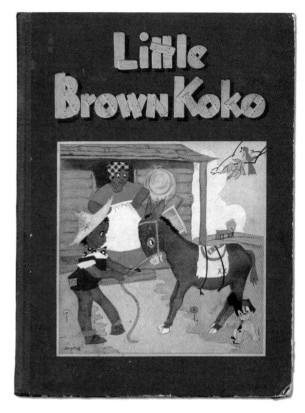

taboo, but they occurred often. All black women and girls, regardless of their physical appearances, were vulnerable to being sexually assaulted by white men. The mammy caricature tells many lies; in this case, the lie is that white men did not find black women sexually desirable.

The mammy caricature implied that black women were only fit to be domestic workers; thus, the stereotype became a rationalization for economic discrimination. During the Jim Crow period, approximately 1877 to 1966, America's race-based, race-segregated job economy limited most blacks to menial, low-paying, and low-status jobs. Many black women ·found themselves forced into one job category, house servant. Jo Ann Gibson Robinson, a biographer of the civil rights movement, described the limited opportunities for black women in the 1950s: "Jobs for clerks in dime stores, cashiers in markets, and telephone operators were numerous, but were not open to black women. A fifty-dollar-a-week worker could employ a black domestic to clean her home, cook the food, wash and iron clothes, and nurse the baby for as little as twenty dollars per week."[3] During slavery only the very wealthy could afford to "purchase" black women and use them as house servants, but during the Jim Crow era even middle-class white women could hire black domestic workers. These black women were not mammies. Mammy was "black, fat with huge

ABOVE 1931 edition of *The Story of Little Black Sambo*, 1940 edition of *Little Brown Koko*.
RIGHT: All of the common caricatures of blacks were represented in games. Players, often children, received messages through a game's graphics and text that blacks were lazy or deviant—and deserved to be mocked or hurt. This game

64 is from the 1880s.

Little Black Sambo

home to Black Mumbo for her to cook with."

So he put it all into the great big brass pot and took it home to Black Mumbo to cook with.

When Black Mumbo saw the melted butter, wasn't she pleased! "Now," said she, "we'll all have pancakes for supper!"

So she got flour and eggs and milk and sugar and butter, and she made a huge big plate of most lovely pancakes. And she fried them in the melted butter which the Tigers had made, and they were just as yellow and brown as little Tigers.

30

breasts, and head covered with a kerchief to hide her nappy hair, strong, kind, loyal, sexless, religious and superstitious."[4] She spoke bastardized English and did not care about her appearance. She was politically and culturally safe. She was, of course, a figment of the white imagination, a nostalgic yearning for a reality that never had been. The real-life black domestic workers of the Jim Crow era were poor women denied other opportunities. They performed many of the duties of the fictional mammies, but, unlike the caricature, they were dedicated to their own families, and often resentful of their lowly societal status.

Fictional Mammies

The slavery-era mammy did not want to be free. She was too busy serving as surrogate mother/grandmother to white families. Mammy was so loyal to her white family that she was often willing to risk her life to defend them. In D.W. Griffith's movie *The Birth of a Nation*—based on Thomas Dixon's racist novel *The Clansman*—the mammy defends her white master's home against black and white Union soldiers. The message was clear: Mammy would rather fight than be free. In the movie *Gone with the Wind*, the black mammy also fights black soldiers whom she believes to be a threat to the white mistress of the house.[5]

Mammy found life on vaudeville stages, in novels, in plays, and finally in films and on television. White men, wearing black face makeup, performed vaudeville skits as Sambos, mammies, and other antiblack stereotypes. The standard for mammy depictions was offered by Harriet Beecher Stowe's 1852 book, *Uncle Tom's Cabin*. The book's mammy, Aunt Chloe, is described in this way:

> A round, black, shiny face is hers, so glossy as to suggest the idea that she might have been washed over with the whites of eggs, like one of her own tea rusks. Her whole plump countenance beams with satisfaction and contentment from under a well-starched checked turban, bearing on it, however, if we must confess it, a little of that tinge of self-consciousness which becomes the first cook of the neighborhood, as Aunt Chloe was universally held and acknowledged to be.[6]

Aunt Chloe was nurturing and protective of her white family, but less caring toward her own children. She is the prototypical fictional mammy: self-sacrificing, white-identified, fat, asexual, good-humored, a loyal cook, housekeeper, and quasi-family member.

During the first half of the 1900s, while black Americans were demanding political, social, and economic advancement, Mammy was increasingly popular in the field of entertainment. The first feature-length

This 1910 edition of *The Story of Little Black Sambo* (Reilly & Britton) was one of the many knockoffs of Helen Bannerman's 1899 original. **67**

sound film was 1927's *The Jazz Singer* with Al Jolson in blackface singing "My Mammy."[7] In 1934 the movie *Imitation of Life* told the story of a black maid, Aunt Delilah (played by Louise Beavers) who inherited a pancake recipe. This movie mammy gave the valuable recipe to Miss Bea, her boss. Miss Bea successfully marketed the recipe. She offered Aunt Delilah a 20 percent interest in the pancake company.[8]

> "You'll have your own car. Your own house," Miss Bea tells Aunt Delilah. Mammy is frightened. "My own house? You gonna send me away, Miss Bea? I can't live with you? Oh, Honey Chile, please don't send me away." Aunt Delilah, though she had lived her entire life in poverty, does not want her own house. "How I gonna take care of you and Miss Jessie (Miss Bea's daughter) if I ain't here . . . I'se your cook. And I want to stay your cook." Regarding the pancake recipe, Aunt Delilah said, "I gives it to you, Honey. I makes you a present of it."[9]

Aunt Delilah worked to keep the white family stable, but her own family disintegrated—her self-hating daughter rejected her, then ran away from home to "pass for white." Near the movie's conclusion, Aunt Delilah dies "of a broken heart."

Imitation of Life was probably the highlight of Louise Beavers's acting career. Almost all of her characters, before and after the Aunt Delilah role, were mammies or mammy-like. She played hopelessly naive maids in Mae West's *She Done Him Wrong*, and Jean Harlow's *Bombshell*. She played loyal servants in *Made for Each Other*, *Mr. Blandings Builds His Dream House*, and several other movies.[10] Beavers had a weight problem: it was a constant battle for her to stay overweight. She often wore padding to give her the appearance of a mammy. Also, she had been reared in California, and she had to fabricate a southern accent. Moreover, she detested cooking. She was truly a fictional mammy.

Imitation of Life was remade (without the pancake recipe storyline) in 1959.[11] It starred Lana Turner as the white mistress, and Juanita Moore (in an Oscar-nominated Best Supporting Actress performance) as the mammy. It was also a tear-jerker.

Hattie McDaniel was another well-known mammy portrayer. In her early films, for example *The Golden West* and *The Story of Temple Drake*, she played unobtrusive, weak mammies. However, her role in *Judge Priest* signaled the beginning of the sassy, quick-tempered mammies that she popularized. She played the saucy mammy in many movies, including *Music Is Magic*, *The Little Colonel*, *Alice Adams*, *Saratoga*, and *The Mad Miss Manton*. In 1939, she played Scarlett O'Hara's sassy but loyal servant in *Gone with the Wind*. She won an Oscar for Best Supporting Actress,

Black children have been portrayed as picaninnies in many books, including *Topsy Turvy and the Easter Bunny* (1939), *All about Little Black Sambo* (1917), and *What Happened to Squash-Boo* (1922).

68

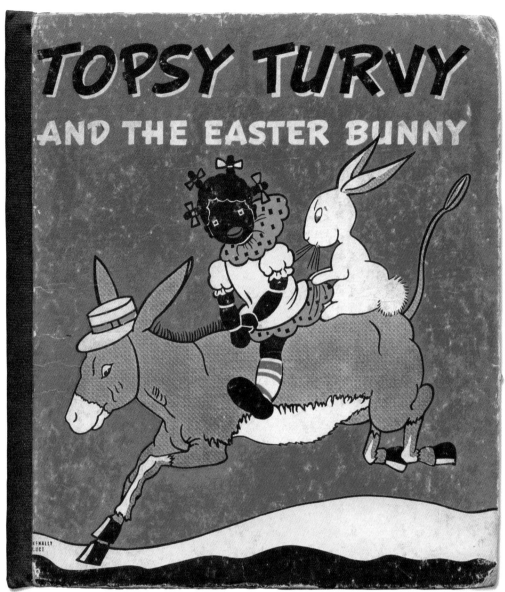

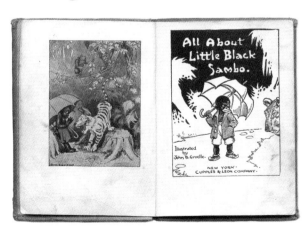

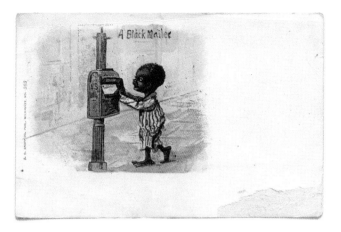

the first black to win an Academy Award.[12] McDaniel was a gifted actress who added depth to the character of mammy; unfortunately, she, like almost all blacks from the 1920s through 1950s, was typecast as a servant. When criticized for perpetuating the mammy caricature, she responded this way: "Why should I complain about making seven thousand dollars a week playing a maid? If I didn't, I'd be making seven dollars a week actually being one."[13]

Beulah was a television show, popular from 1950 to 1953, in which a mammy nurtures a white suburban family. Hattie McDaniel originated the role for radio; Louise Beavers performed the role on television. The Beulah image resurfaced in the 1980s when Nell Carter, a talented black singer, played a mammy-like role on the situation comedy *Gimme a Break*. She was dark-skinned, overweight, sassy, white-identified, and, like Aunt Delilah in *Imitation of Life*, content to live in her white employer's home and nurture the white family.

Commercial Mammies

Mammy was born on the plantation in the imagination of slavery defenders, but she grew in popularity during the period of Jim Crow. The

LEFT: Postcard, postmarked 1906.
TOP RIGHT: Postcard, postmarked 1911.
BOTTOM RIGHT: Postcard, postmarked 1906.

Me Fo'get You? NEBER! Fo' Ah Likes you MORE DAN EBER! BE MY VALENTINE!

© 5292 C U.S.A.

mainstreaming of Mammy was primarily, but not exclusively, the result of the fledgling advertising industry. The mammy image was used to sell many household items, especially breakfast foods, detergents, planters, ashtrays, sewing accessories, and beverages. As early as 1875, Aunt Sally, a mammy image, appeared on cans of baking powder. Later, different mammy images appeared on Luzianne coffee and cleaners, Fun to Wash detergent, Aunt Dinah molasses, and other products. Mammy represented wholesomeness. You can trust the mammy pitchwoman.

Mammy's most successful commercial expression was, and still is, Aunt Jemima. In 1889, Charles Rutt, a Missouri newspaper editor, and Charles G. Underwood, a mill owner, developed the idea of a self-rising flour that only needed water. He called it Aunt Jemima's recipe. They borrowed the Aunt Jemima name from a popular vaudeville song that he had heard performed by a team of minstrel performers. The minstrels

This 1940s Valentine's card demeans romantic relations involving African Americans.

71

"Topsy" was a song made popular by the sisters Rosetta and Vivian Duncan, an American vaudeville duo. The sheet music is from 1924.

included a skit with a southern mammy. Rutt decided to use the name and the image of the mammy-like Aunt Jemima to promote his new pancake mix. Unfortunately for him, he and his partner lacked the necessary capital to effectively promote and market the product. They sold the pancake recipe and the accompanying Aunt Jemima marketing idea to the R.T. Davis Mill Company.

The R.T. Davis Company improved the pancake formula and, more importantly, they developed an advertising plan to use a real person to portray Aunt Jemima. The woman they found to serve as the live model was Nancy Green, who was born a slave in Kentucky in 1834.

She impersonated Aunt Jemima until her death in 1923. Struggling to make money, the R.T. Davis Company made the bold decision to risk their entire fortune and future on a promotional exhibition at the 1893 World's Exposition in Chicago. They constructed the world's largest flour barrel, twenty-four feet high and twelve feet across. Standing near the barrel, Nancy Green, dressed as Aunt Jemima, sang songs, cooked pancakes, and told stories about the Old South—stories which presented the South as a happy place for blacks and whites alike. She was a huge success. She had served tens of thousands of pancakes by the time the fair ended. Her success established her as a national celebrity. Her image was plastered on billboards nationwide, with the caption, "I'se in town, honey." Green, in her role as Aunt Jemima, made appearances at countless country fairs, flea markets, food shows, and local grocery stores. By the turn of the century, Aunt Jemima and the Armour meat chef were the two commercial symbols most trusted by American housewives.[14] By 1910 more than 120 million Aunt Jemima breakfasts were being served annually. The popularity of Aunt Jemima inspired many giveaway and mail-in premiums, including dolls, breakfast club pins, dishware, and recipe booklets.

The R.T. Davis Mill Company was renamed the Aunt Jemima Mills Company in 1914 and sold to the Quaker Oats Company in 1926. In 1933 Anna Robinson, who weighed 350 pounds, became the second Aunt Jemima. She was much heavier and darker in complexion than was Nancy Green. The third Aunt Jemima was Edith Wilson, who is known primarily for playing the role of Aunt Jemima on radio and television shows between 1948 and 1966. By the 1960s the Quaker Oats Company was a market leader in the breakfast business, and Aunt Jemima was an American icon. In recent years, Aunt Jemima has been given a makeover: her skin is lighter and the handkerchief has been removed from her head. She now has the appearance of an attractive maid—not a Jim Crow–era mammy.

Tom: Mammy's Male Counterpart

The Tom caricature portrays black men as faithful, happily submissive servants. The Tom caricature, like the mammy caricature, was born in antebellum America in the defense of slavery. How could slavery be wrong, argued its proponents, if black servants, males (Toms) and females (mammies), were contented and loyal? The Tom is presented as a smiling, wide-eyed, dark-skinned server: fieldworker, cook, butler, porter, or waiter. Tom is portrayed as a dependable worker, eager to serve. He is docile and nonthreatening to whites. The Tom is often old, physically weak, and psychologically dependent on whites for approval. Donald

Bogle summarizes the depiction of toms in movies: "Always as toms are chased, harassed, hounded, flogged, enslaved, and insulted, they keep the faith, n'er turn against their white massas, and remain hearty, submissive, stoic, generous, selfless, and oh-so-very kind. Thus they endear themselves to white audiences and emerge as heroes of sorts."[15]

In some ways Bogle's description is similar to the portrayal of the main black character in *Uncle Tom's Cabin*. Stowe's Tom is a gentle, humble, Christian slave. His faith is simple, natural, and complete. Stowe uses Tom's character to show the perfect gentleness and forgiving nature which she believed lay dormant in all blacks. These qualities reveal themselves under favorable conditions. Mr. Shelby, Tom's first enslaver, is sympathetic; therefore, Tom's innate spirituality flourishes. Mr. Shelby is not a good businessman; his financial troubles necessitate that he sell Tom. Tom does not run away despite a warning that he is to be sold. Mr. St. Clare, his second enslaver, befriends Tom and promises to free him. Unfortunately for Tom, Mr. St. Clare is killed before signing manumission papers. Tom's fortunes take a decidedly downward turn. Tom is sold to Simon Legree, a brutal and sadistic deep South plantation owner. Legree is also a drunkard who hates religion and religious people.

Legree intends to make Tom an overseer. Tom is ordered by Legree to flog a woman slave. Tom refuses. Legree strikes him repeatedly with a cowhide lash. Again, he tells Tom to beat the woman. Tom, with a soft voice, says, "the poor crittur's sick and feeble; 'twould be downright cruel, and it's what I never would do, nor begin to. Mas'r, if you mean to kill me, kill me; but, as to my raising my hand agin anyone here, I never shall,— I'll die first."[16]

Images of the Tom caricature found on a matchbook from the 1920s and a 1910 postcard.

Greetings from SHREVE, OHIO

Stowe wanted to show how slavery was incongruent with Christianity. How could Christians, she wondered, buy, sell, and trade people? How could they offer even tacit approval of slavery? How could white Christians allow their enslaved brethren to be sold to the likes of Legree? Her book is an unabashed attack on slavery, and Tom is one of her two perfect Christian characters; Mr. St. Clare's daughter, Eva, the other. Both die, Tom as a martyr.

Legree demands information from Tom about two women runaways. He knows that Tom can help him. Tom refuses. Legree beats Tom and threatens to kill him if Tom does not help him find the women. Tom, ever the Christian, does not lie, nor does he give Legree the information. Instead, Tom says:

> Mas'r, if you was sick, or in trouble, or dying, and I could save ye, I'd give ye my heart's blood; and if taking every drop of blood in this poor old body would save your precious soul, I'd give 'em freely, as the Lord gave His for me. O, Mas'r! don't bring this great sin on your soul! It will hurt you more than 'twill me! Do the worst you can, my troubles'll be over soon; but if ye don't repent, yours won't never end.[17]

Postcard of a happy Tom, date unknown.

Legree beats Tom; Sambo, one of Legree's black overseers, flogs Tom. As Tom is dying, Legree yells to Sambo, "Give it to him!" Tom opens his eyes, looks at Legree, and says, "Ye poor miserable crittur! There ain't no more that ye can do! I forgive ye, with all my soul."[18] Soon afterward, Tom dies. Stowe portrayed him as a Christ figure, albeit a childlike one. Tom was offered as a sacrifice for the sins of an evil institution.

Despite being a model slave—hardworking, loyal, nonrebellious, and often contented—Tom is sold, cursed, slapped, kicked, flogged, worked like a horse, then beaten to death. He never lifts a hand to hit his enslavers or to stop a blow. Tom does not complain, rebel, or run away. This partially explains why the names "Uncle Tom" and "Tom" have become terms of disgust for African Americans. Tom's devotion to his enslaver is surpassed only by his devotion to his religious faith.

Uncle Tom's Cabin sold over two million copies within two years of its publication in 1853. In the first three years after its publication, fourteen proslavery novels were written to contradict the book's antislavery messages. Stowe's portrayal of slavery was also undermined on entertainment stages. By 1879 there were at least forty-nine traveling companies performing *Uncle Tom's Cabin* throughout the United States.[19] The stage versions, often called Tom shows, differed from Stowe's book in significant ways. Little Eva was now the star; all other characters were relegated to the periphery. The violence inherent in slavery was understated. In some instances the brutality was ignored completely. Slaves were depicted as "happy darkies" living under a benevolent, paternalistic system. Legree was mean but not a sadist, and in some Tom shows he was portrayed as doing Tom a favor by killing him because Tom could not enter heaven unless he died.

The stage Toms represented a major, and demeaning, departure from the original Uncle Tom. Stowe's Tom was an obedient, loyal, noncomplaining slave, but he was not physically or morally weak. Tom resisted Legree. He gave his life rather than help Legree find the two women runaways. Stowe portrayed Tom as a man with dignity—an enslaved man who dared to pity his enslavers. Throughout the novel, Tom is venerable and kind. His theology, though simple, is fully developed and consistent. He is a man of principle. Patricia Turner wrote:

> Further marked inconsistencies are discernible between the values and principles of the reconstructed Uncle Tom and Stowe's original hero. Both are devout, stalwart Christians. Both are unflinching in their loyalty. But the reconstructed Uncle Toms are passive, docile, unthinking Christians. Loyal and faithful to white employers, they are duplicitous in their dealings with fellow blacks. Stowe's Tom is

Liberty Magazine, May 10, 1941, with portrayal of black man as Tom or coon.

a proactive Christian warrior. He does more than accept God's will, he endeavors to fulfill it in all of his words and deeds. He is loyal to each of his white masters, even the cruel Simon Legree. Yet his allegiance to his fellow slaves is equally strong.[20]

The versions of Uncle Tom that entertained audiences on stages were drained of these noble traits. He was an unthinking religious slave, sometimes happy, often fearful. Significantly, the stage Toms were middle-aged or elderly. He was shown stooped, often with a cane or stick. He was thin, almost emaciated. His eyesight was failing. These depictions of Uncle Tom are inconsistent with Stowe's Tom who was a "broad-chested, strong-armed fellow." Stowe's original was the father of small children, unlike the desexed Toms of the stage. Stowe's Tom was capable of outworking most slaves. Patricia Turner says of Stowe, "By depicting his ability to save a child's life and work long days in the field, she delivers a brave, physically capable hero whose abilities contradict the lazy slave stereotype then being actively promoted by pro-slavery Southerners. The elderly, stooped-over, slow-moving Uncle Tom of contemporary popular culture could never have fulfilled the political ends sought by Stowe."[21]

Cinematic Uncle Toms

Portrayals of Uncle Tom in movies also departed from Stowe's original. In 1903, Edwin S. Porter directed a twelve-minute version of *Uncle Tom's Cabin*. This was the first black character in an American film; poignantly, Uncle Tom was played by an unnamed white actor colored with blackface makeup. Porter's Uncle Tom, like the Toms on stage, was a childlike, groveling servant. In the first quarter of the twentieth century there were many cinematic adaptations of *Uncle Tom's Cabin* which portrayed slavery as a benevolent institution, Little Eva as an earthly angel, and blacks, especially Tom, as loyal, childlike, unthinking, and happy. In 1914, a black actor, Sam Lucas, was allowed to play the Uncle Tom role in a film. His advanced age—he was seventy-two—helped perpetuate the perception that Uncle Tom was old and physically weak. In 1927 Universal Pictures remade *Uncle Tom's Cabin* and used the black actor James B. Lowe in the title role. The Toms played by Lucas and Lowe, like the many Toms played by white actors in blackface makeup, were genial, passive, happy servants.[22]

Uncle Tom was not the only Tom depicted in early American movies. Indeed, the Tom character was a staple of the movie screen and, later, television shows. In the silent short film *Confederate Spy*, Uncle Daniel, a Tom character, is a southern black spy. He is caught and brought before a Union firing squad. He has no regrets facing death because he "did it for

This 1940s postcard from the Asheville Post Card Company both derides and warns black Americans.

ND-154

The Darkey Preacher

―――

"Listen Sistern and Bredren,
You must give up your devilish
  way
Give up all your wickedness,
Or de good Lawd'll make you
  pay

Stop drinking dat mean corn
  likker,
Dat makes you crazy to fight.
Stop rolling dose "Galloping
  dominoes",
Dat makes you stay up all
  night.

Sisters, don't let your tongues
  wag too much,
Stop putting on all dat paint.
And don't use dat bleach and
  powder,
Dat makes you look white when
  you ain't.

Before we dismiss, we'll jine
  in prayer
De deacons will now pass the
  plates aroun,
And if you don't help out de
  collection,
St. Peter will mos likely turn
  you down." ©

Verse Copyrighted by Asheville Post Card Co.

E-6577

massa's sake and for little massa." In *For Massa's Sake*, a former slave is so attached to his former master that he sells himself back into slavery to help pay the white man's debts. *The Birth of a Nation* and *Hearts in Dixie* have numerous antiblack caricatures, including Toms who adore their masters.[23]

In the 1930s and 1940s, black male actors were limited to two stereotypical roles: coons—lazy buffoons—such as Stepin Fetchit, Mantan Moreland, and Willie Best; and Toms, of whom the most notable were Bill "Bojangles" Robinson, Clarence Muse, and Eddie "Rochester" Anderson. Robinson is best known as child star Shirley Temple's dance partner. They appeared in four films together, including *The Littlest Rebel*. Robinson plays the role of Uncle Billy, a good-natured, well-mannered Tom. Temple plays Virginia Houston Cary, the feisty young daughter of Captain Cary of the Confederate Army. Captain Cary goes off to battle. The Cary plantation is invaded by Union soldiers. Virginia's mother becomes ill and soon dies. Captain Cary returns home and is taken prisoner. He is tried for treason. Uncle Billy helps little Virginia escape. The pair earns their fare to Washington by dancing and "passing the cap." Miraculously, they gain an audience with President Abraham Lincoln who pardons Virginia's father. Robinson also portrayed genial, loyal servants in *The Little Colonel* with Temple and Lionel Barrymore, *In Old Kentucky* with Will Rogers, and *Just Around the Corner* with Temple.[24]

Clarence Muse was a graduate of the Dickinson School of Law in Philadelphia and he had formal theatrical training; nevertheless, his career is noted for portrayals of coons and Toms, especially the latter. He played Tom roles in *Show Boat*, *Follow Your Heart*, *Zanzibar*, *Heaven Can Wait*, *Joe Palooka in the Knockout*, and *Riding High*. The Tom role, like most of the early black stereotypes, suggested that blacks were one-dimensional. Muse's Toms were thoughtful and often articulate servants. Bogle calls him the "dignified, humanized tom."[25]

Eddie Anderson played the Tom role in *Jezebel* and *You Can't Cheat an Honest Man*, but he is best known as Jack Benny's raspy voiced manservant Rochester. The pair appeared in movies, for example *Love Thy Neighbor* and *The Meanest Man in the World*, radio programs, and a long-running television program. Their on-screen relationship was characterized by good-natured struggles, with Rochester often besting his "Boss." Rochester was one of the first black characters to "show up" his white employer; but the character was a Tom, albeit with elements of shrewdness.[26]

The 1930s and 1940s were the heyday for cinematic Tom depictions. Virtually every film that dealt with slavery included Toms. The still popular *Gone with the Wind* included the Tom character Pork, a pathetic man, his back stooped, his speech halted, afraid of whites, yet desiring,

A postcard, postmarked 1907, showing the talented black servant. **81**

above all, to please them. Pork is a marginal character. In later movies Toms would be even more marginalized, many lacking names. Coons played the role of comic relief. Toms symbolized wealth. Producers who wanted to show that a family had "old money" often surrounded the family with black servants. Cinematic Toms represented nostalgic yearnings for the supposed "good ol' days" before the civil rights and black power movements.

Sidney Poitier, the leading black male actor of the 1960s, also played roles that approximated the Tom stereotype, even though his characters were never one-dimensional. Poitier did not play characters that were submissive, cheerful servants, but many of his characters were white-identified. In *Edge of the City* Poitier sacrifices his life, and in *The Defiant Ones* he sacrifices his freedom, for white males. Like the black servants of old, his characters work to improve the lives of whites. In *Lilies of the Field* he helps refugee nuns build a chapel, in *The Slender Thread* he helps a suicidal white woman, and in *A Patch of Blue* he aids a young blind woman who does not know he is black. In *To Sir, with Love* Poitier tries to teach working-class youth, almost all white, to value education. Some of the students racially taunt him, and eventually he loses his composure. Later, he berates himself for having displayed anger. The reluctance to fight back is reminiscent of earlier Tom portrayals, for example Bill Robinson's character in *The Little Colonel*, who stands patiently and silently as he is insulted by the white master. Bogle describes Poitier's roles this way:

> They were mild-mannered toms, throwbacks to the humanized Christian servants of the 1930s. When insulted or badgered, the Poitier character stood by and took it. He knew the white world meant him no real harm. He differed from the old servants only in that he was governed by a code of decency, duty, and moral intelligence. There were times in his films when he screamed out in rage at the injustices of a racist white society. But reason always dictated his actions, along with love for his fellow man.[27]

Poitier's characters, like earlier Toms, were also denied sex lives. In many of his roles he has no wife or girlfriend, and when he did have romantic relationships, they were drained of sexual tension and fulfillment. In *A Raisin in the Sun* there are no romantic scenes with his black wife. In *Guess Who's Coming to Dinner* he only kisses his white fiancée once, and the audience sees the kiss through a cabdriver's rear view mirror.[28] In *A Patch of Blue* he kisses the white romantic interest once, and then sacrifices any amorous possibilities by arranging for her to leave for a school for the blind.[29]

Possible creamer, 1940s.   **83**

Poitier's Toms are best described as "Enlightened Toms." In many of his films he is the smartest, most articulate character—and, more importantly, the one who delves into the philosophical issues: egalitarianism, humanitarianism, and altruism. Moreover, he acts upon these philosophical musings. He is a paragon of saintly virtue, sacrificing for others, who, not coincidentally, are often white.

Morgan Freeman's character, Hoke, in *Driving Miss Daisy* is reminiscent of Poitier's Homer Smith in *Lilies of the Field*. Neither Hoke nor Homer has a life apart from whites. We know little of either character's experiences or hopes. They live to solve the problems of the white characters; and, of course, both are desexed. Although neither is a fully developed character, both are preferable to Big George in *Fried Green Tomatoes*. Big George is a pliant, obedient, one-dimensional servant, a relic.[30]

The Tom caricature resurfaced in Quentin Tarantino's movie, *Django Unchained*.[31] Stephen, the Tom portrayed by Samuel L. Jackson, is in some ways reminiscent of earlier Toms: old, physically impaired, a groveler. Yet unlike almost all cinematic portrayals of Toms, Stephen is a cruel and contemptible opportunist. He not only loves whites—especially his enslaver—but he loathes blacks.

In contemporary America, "Uncle Tom" is a slur used to disparage a black person who is humiliatingly subservient to white people; it is often used by blacks against other blacks. In some instances it is used to describe a black person who is a docile, loyal, religious, contented servant who accommodates himself to a lowly status. More often, it is used in reference to an ambitious black person who subordinates himself in order to achieve personal gain. The Tom character in *Django Unchained* represents the latter—and may be seen as Tarantino bringing a modern interpretation of Tom to the cinema. Stephen is almost wholly lacking in redemptive qualities: he is a groveling, conniving, unscrupulous opportunist who brutalizes black people to gain benefits and soothe his self-hatred.

Commercial Toms

The list of Toms who have been used to sell products is too long to exhaust here. In the 1890s Dixon's Carburet of Iron Stove Polish used "Uncle Obadiah" in their advertisements. He is elderly, frail, with ragged clothes, but he is smiling. In the 1920s Schulze Baking Company used the image of an old banjo-strumming Tom on its advertisement selling Uncle Wabash Cupcakes. In the 1940s Listerine used a black porter in its magazine advertisements, and Mil-Kay Vitamin Drinks used a smiling black waiter on its posters and billboards. A 1950s souvenir tip tray from The Homestead in Hot Springs, Virginia, shows a smiling black waiter

"A ROW OF PALMS"—IN FLORIDA

balancing plates on his head. In the 1940s Converted Rice changed the name of its major product to Uncle Ben's Brand Rice, and began using the image of a smiling, elderly black man on its package.

Arguably the most enduring commercial Tom is "Rastus," the Cream of Wheat cook.

Rastus was created in 1893 by Emery Mapes, one of the owners of North Dakota's Diamond Milling Company.[32] He wanted a likable image to help sell packages of breakfast porridge. Mapes, a former printer, remembered the image of a black chef among his stock of old printing blocks. He made a template of the chef and named the product Cream of Wheat. The original logo showed a black chef holding a skillet in one hand and a bowl of Cream of Wheat in the other.[33] This logo was used until the 1920s when Mapes, impressed by the "wholesome" looks of a Chicago waiter serving him breakfast, created a new chef. The waiter was paid five dollars to pose as the second Rastus in a chef's hat and jacket. The image of this unknown man has appeared, with only slight modifications, on Cream of Wheat boxes for almost ninety years.

Rastus, like Aunt Jemima, is more than a company trademark—he is a cultural icon. Rastus is marketed as a symbol of wholeness and sta- bility. The toothy, well-dressed black chef happily serves breakfast to

A postcard, postmarked 1924, with black men as indistinguishable Toms.

a nation. In 1898 Cream of Wheat began advertising in national magazines. These advertisements were often reproduced as posters. Many of those advertisements are, by today's standards, racially insensitive. For example, a 1915 Cream of Wheat poster shows "Uncle Sam" looking at a picture of Rastus holding a bowl of the cereal. The caption reads "Well, You're Helping Some!" This may have been a suggestion that blacks were not significant contributors to the war effort. A 1921 Cream of Wheat poster shows a young white boy sitting in a rickshaw that is being pulled by an elderly black man. The man has stopped to smoke. The smiling boy, waving a whip-like stick, says, "Giddap, Uncle." Often Rastus is portrayed as barely literate. In a 1921 advertisement, Rastus, smiling, his gums showing, holds a sign which reads:

> Maybe Cream of Wheat
> aint got no vitamines.
> I dont know what them
> things is. If they's bugs
> they aint none in Cream of
> Wheat but she's sho' good
> to eat and cheap. Costs 'bout
> 1¢ fo a great big dish.

Uncle Tom as Opprobrium

"Uncle Tom," unlike most antiblack slurs, is primarily used by blacks against blacks. Its synonyms include "oreo," "sell-out," "uncle," "race-traitor," and "white man's negro." It is an in-group term used as a social control mechanism. Garth Baker-Fletcher wrote, "The 'Uncle Tom' appellation is the feared curse of every African American who is compelled to work under whites, while simultaneously holding a position of authority over other African Americans. Thus 'Uncle Tom' can be pulled out by blacks as a superior ideological weapon to enforce patterns of racial unity against the perceived threats of a white boss."[34]

Civil rights leaders of the 1960s were called Uncle Toms by more militant blacks. Whitney Young, executive director of the Urban League from 1961 to 1971, was an ardent integrationist. His willingness to work with whites led to charges that he was an Uncle Tom. Reverend Martin Luther King Jr.'s unwillingness to advocate retaliatory violence led Stokely Carmichael to accuse him of "Uncle Tomism." Bayard Rustin, one of the chief tacticians of the civil rights movement, was also called an Uncle Tom by black militants.[35] Roy Wilkins was called an Uncle Tom because he publicly stated that blacks could achieve political power "in the system."

Today, black political conservatives, especially Republicans, are often labeled Uncle Toms or "Toms." Supreme Court Justice Clarence Thomas; Alan Keyes, the Republican presidential candidate; Shelby Steele, the professor and author; Thomas Sowell, the economist; and Walter Williams, the neighborhood activist, have all been publicly called Uncle Toms. They are accused of being white-identified opportunists. Their motives are impugned. The November 1996 issue of *Emerge* magazine had a cover with Justice Thomas dressed as a lawn jockey and the words "Uncle Thomas, Lawn Jockey for the Far Right."[36] Inside the magazine a grinning Justice Thomas shines Associate Justice Antonin Scalia's shoes.

Black public figures who advocate conservative positions are often accused of pleasing whites only to elevate themselves—socially, politically, and economically. They publicly say about race what conservative whites dare not say: crime and welfare are black phenomena, affirmative action is reverse discrimination, and white racism is not the cause of black problems. They wear the "Uncle Tom" label as a badge of pride—at least publicly. To their opponents these men represent Uncle Toms.

Noted black athletes, especially those who publicly express conservative political views, run the risk of being labeled Uncle Toms. After retiring

Postcard, copyrighted 1951, by Tichnor Brothers Inc.

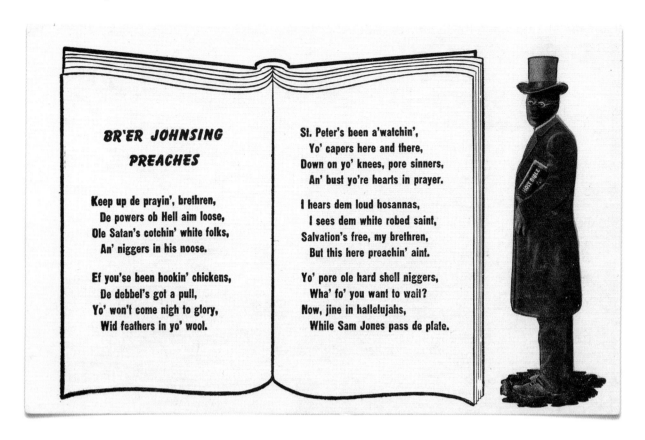

BR'ER JOHNSING PREACHES

Keep up de prayin', brethren,
 De powers ob Hell aim loose,
Ole Satan's cotchin' white folks,
 An' niggers in his noose.

Ef you'se been hookin' chickens,
 De debbel's got a pull,
Yo' won't come nigh to glory,
 Wid feathers in yo' wool.

St. Peter's been a'watchin',
 Yo' capers here and there,
Down on yo' knees, pore sinners,
 An' bust yo're hearts in prayer.

I hears dem loud hosannas,
 I sees dem white robed saint,
Salvation's free, my brethren,
 But this here preachin' aint.

Yo' pore ole hard shell niggers,
 Wha' fo' you want to wait?
Now, jine in hallelujahs,
 While Sam Jones pass de plate.

from baseball, Jackie Robinson wrote a newspaper column about civil rights issues. He was vilified in the black community when he announced that he was a "Rockefeller Republican." Arthur Ashe, the tennis champion and human rights activist, was called an Uncle Tom for playing in the South African Open tennis tournament in 1973. His participation was seen as supporting apartheid. Muhammad Ali routinely berated his black opponents as Uncle Toms. In 1965 Ali fought Floyd Patterson, a devout Christian and staunch integrationist. Patterson used these words to criticize Ali for becoming a Black Muslim:

> Cassius Clay [Ali's former name] is disgracing himself and the Negro race. No decent person can look up to a champion whose credo is "hate whites." I have nothing but contempt for the Black Muslims and that for which they stand. The image of a Black Muslim as the world heavyweight champion disgraces the sport and the nation. Cassius Clay must be beaten and the Black Muslims' scourge removed from boxing.[37]

Ali not only called Patterson an "Uncle Tom" and "the technicolor white hope," but he predicted: "I'm gonna put him flat on his back, so that he will start acting black; because when he was champ he didn't do as he should, he tried to force himself into an all-white neighborhood."[38] During the fight—a one-sided bout—Ali toyed with Patterson. Ali threw both punches and the slur "white nigger."

In February 1967, Ali's opponent was Ernie Terrell. At the prefight press conferences Terrell repeatedly called Ali by his given name: Cassius Clay. Ali promised to beat Terrell until he addressed him properly.[39] In a fight that *Sports Illustrated* described as "a wonderful demonstration of boxing skill and a barbarous display of cruelty," Ali beat Terrell while shouting, "What's my name, 'Uncle Tom,' what's my name?"[40] Before their first fight, on March 8, 1971, Ali called Joe Frazier an "Uncle Tom" and said that whites would be cheering for Frazier. He also used the slur against Joe Louis because of Louis's passive political stances.

In recent years the "Uncle Tom" slur has been directed against Christopher Darden, the black member of the prosecution's team in the O.J. Simpson murder trial; Detroit Mayor Dennis Archer; Karl Malone, the Utah Jazz basketball player; and Colin Powell. In *The Fab Five*, a 2011 ESPN film about the University of Michigan basketball careers of Jalen Rose, Juwan Howard, Chris Webber, Jimmy King, and Ray Jackson from 1991 to 1993, Rose, the show's executive producer, stated that Duke University recruited only black players he considered to be "Uncle Toms."[41] Cornel West, the author of *Race Matters* and a lifelong civil rights activist, was called an Uncle Tom by the African United Front because of his "support" of Jews, and he and Tavis Smiley were called Uncle Toms in 2012 for their criticism of President Obama.[42] Even W.E.B. Du Bois, arguably the greatest, most sustained civil rights voice of the twentieth century, was called an Uncle Tom—by Marcus Garvey, who added that Du Bois was "purely and simply a white man's nigger."

The "Uncle Tom" slur has been appropriated by other ethnic groups to exert in-group pressures on their members. A Native American, for example, who is believed to be too friendly with or admiring of whites, is called an "Uncle Tomahawk"; Chinese Americans have used the term "Uncle Tong."

Picaninny

The picaninny was the dominant racial caricature of black children for most of this country's history.[43] They were "child coons," miniature versions of Stepin Fetchit.[44] Picaninnies had bulging eyes, unkempt hair, red lips, and wide mouths into which they stuffed huge slices of watermelon. They were themselves tasty morsels for alligators. They were routinely shown on postcards, posters, and other ephemera being chased or eaten. Picaninnies were portrayed as nameless, shiftless natural buffoons running from alligators and toward fried chicken.

The first famous picaninny was Topsy—a poorly dressed, disreputable, neglected enslaved girl—who appeared in Stowe's *Uncle Tom's Cabin*. She was created to show the evils of slavery. Here was an untamable "wild child" who had been indelibly corrupted by slavery.

> She was one of the blackest of her race; and her round, shining eyes, glittering as glass beads, moved with quick and restless glances over everything in the room. Her mouth half open with astonishment at the wonders of the new Mas'r's parlor, displayed a white and brilliant set of teeth. Her woolly hair was braided in sundry little tails, which stuck out in every direction. The expression of her face was an odd mixture of shrewdness and cunning, over which was oddly drawn, like a veil, an expression of the most doleful gravity and solemnity. She was dressed in a single filthy, ragged garment, made of bagging; and stood with her hands demurely folded in front of her. Altogether, there was something odd and goblin-like about her appearance—something as Miss Ophelia afterwards said, "so heathenish . . ."[45]

Stowe hoped that readers would be heartbroken by the tribulations of Topsy, and would help end slavery—which, she believed, produced many similar children. Her book, while leading some Americans to question the morality of slavery, was used by others to trivialize slavery's brutality. Topsy, for example, was soon a staple character in minstrel shows. The stage Topsy, unlike Stowe's version, was a happy, mirthful character who reveled in her misfortune. Topsy was still dirty, with kinky hair and ragged clothes, but these traits were transformed into comic props—as was her misuse of the English language. No longer a sympathetic figure, Topsy became, simply, a harmless coon. The stage Topsy and her imitators remained popular from the early 1850s well into the twentieth century.[46]

Black children were some of the earliest "stars" of the fledgling motion picture industry, albeit as picaninnies.[47] In 1891 Thomas Alva Edison invented the kinetoscope and the kinetograph, which laid the groundwork for modern motion picture technology. During his camera experiments in 1893, Edison photographed some black children as "interesting side effects." In 1908 he presented *Ten Pickaninnies*,[48] which showed those "side effects" running and playing. These nameless children were referred to as inky kids, smoky kids, black lambs, snowballs, chubbie ebonies, bad chillun, and coons.

Ten Pickaninnies was a forerunner to Hal Roach's Our Gang series of films—sometimes referred to as the Little Rascals. First produced in 1922,[49] Our Gang continued into the talkie era. Roach described the series

The narrative that black children are alligator bait is apparent in these postcards from the 1930s.

183   THE HOME STRETCH

ONE MILE

63766

9234   FREE LUNCH IN THE JUNGLE

218 ALLIGATOR AND CHILD IN PALMETTO GROVE, FLORIDA

© Asheville Post Card Co.

I'm just as scairt as I can be,
I'm 'fraid this 'gater's goin' to get me,

Oh, mammy, come and get me soon
Or you wont have no little coon.

94260

as "comedies of child life." It included an interracial cast of children, including, at various times, these black characters: Sunshine Sammy, Pineapple, and Farina in the 1920s, and later, Stymie and Buckwheat. One or two black children appeared in each short episode.

Our Gang is often credited with being "one of Hollywood's few attempts . . . to do better by the Negro."[50] All of the children, blacks and whites, took turns playing nitwits. Donald Bogle wrote: "Indeed, the charming sense of Our Gang was that all of the children were buffoons, forever in scraps and scrapes, forever plagued by setbacks and sidetracks as they set out to have fun, and everyone had his turn at being outwitted."[51] While this is true, the black characters were often buffoons in racially stereotypical ways. They spoke in dialect—*dis, dat, I is, you is, and we is*. Farina, arguably the most famous picaninny of the 1920s, was on more than one occasion shown savagely eating watermelon or chicken. He was also terrified of ghosts—this fear was a persistent theme for adult coons in comedy films. Farina and Buckwheat wore tightly twisted "picaninny pigtails" and old patched gingham clothes which made their sex ambiguous. Buckwheat, the quiet boy with big eyes, has an unenviable distinction: his name is now synonymous with "picaninny." This is due, in large part, to Eddie Murphy's depiction of Buckwheat on *Saturday Night*

Live in the 1980s. Indeed, "picaninny" is today rarely used as a racial slur; it has been replaced by the term "buckwheat."

Characteristics of Picaninnies

Picaninnies as portrayed in material culture have skin coloring ranging from medium brown to dark black—light-skinned picaninnies are rare. They include infants and teenagers, but most appear to be eight to ten years old. Prissy, the inept and hysterical servant girl in *Gone with the Wind* was an exception. She was older than the typical picaninny, but her character was functionally a picaninny. Picaninny girls (and sometimes boys) have hair tied or matted in short stalks that point in all directions; often the boys are bald, their heads shining like metal. The children have big, wide eyes, and oversized mouths—ostensibly to accommodate enormous pieces of watermelon.

The picaninny caricature shows black children as either poorly dressed, wearing ragged, torn, old, and oversized clothes or, worse, they are shown as nude or near-nude. This nudity suggests that black children, and by extension black parents, are not concerned with modesty. The nudity also implies that black parents neglect their children. A loving parent would provide clothing. The nudity of black children suggests that blacks are less civilized than whites, who wear clothes.

The nudity is also problematic because it sexualizes these children. Black children are shown with exposed genitalia and buttocks often without apparent shame. Moreover, the buttocks are often exaggerated in size, that is, black children are shown with the buttocks of adults. The widespread depictions of nudity among black children normalizes their sexual objectification, and, by extension, justifies the sexual abuse of these children.

A disproportionately large number of African American children are poor, but the picaninny caricature suggests that all black children are impoverished. This poverty is evidenced by their ragged clothes. The children are hungry, therefore they steal chickens and watermelon. Like wild animals, the picaninnies often must fend for themselves.

Picaninnies are portrayed in greeting cards, on-stage, and in physical objects as insignificant beings. Stories like *Ten Little Niggers* show black children being rolled over by boulders, chased by alligators, and set on fire.[52] Black children are shown on postcards being attacked by dogs, chickens, pigs, and other animals. This is consistent with the many nineteenth- and twentieth-century pseudoscientific theories which claimed that blacks were destined for extinction. William Smith, a Tulane University professor, published *The Color Line* in 1905.[53] He argued that blacks would die off because the "doom that awaits the Negro has been prepared in like measure for all inferior races."[54] George Fredrickson's *The Black Image in the White Mind* includes an excellent discussion of the "black race will die" theories.[55]

Picaninnies were often depicted side by side with animals. For example, a 1907 postcard showed a black child on his knees looking at a pig. The caption read, "Whose Baby is OO?" A 1930s bisque match holder showed a black baby emerging from an egg while a rooster looks on. On postcards black children were often referred to as coons, monkeys, crows, and opossums. A 1930s pinback showed a bird with the head of a black girl.[56] Picaninnies were "shown crawling on the ground, climbing trees, straddled over logs, or in other ways assuming animal-like postures."[57] The message was this: black children are more animal than human.

Caricaturing black woman as mammies, black men as Toms, and black children as picaninnies served to dismiss the black family as an irrelevant social unit, both deviant and dysfunctional.

CHAPTER FIVE

Flawed Women

A Woman Called Tragic

Lydia Maria Child introduced the literary character that we call the "tragic mulatto"[1] in two short stories: "The Quadroons" (1842) and "Slavery's Pleasant Homes" (1843). She portrayed this light-skinned woman as the offspring of a white slaveholder and his black female slave. This woman's life was indeed tragic. She was ignorant of both her mother's race and her own. She believed herself to be white and free. Her heart was pure, her manners impeccable, her language polished, and her face beautiful. Her father died; her "negro blood" discovered, she was remanded to slavery, deserted by her white lover, and died a victim of slavery and white male violence. A similar portrayal of the near-white mulatto appeared in *Clotel* (1853), a novel written by black abolitionist William Wells Brown.[2]

A century later literary and cinematic portrayals of the tragic mulatto emphasized her personal pathologies: self-hatred, depression, alcoholism, sexual perversion, and suicide attempts being the most common. If light enough to "pass" as white, she did, but passing led to deeper self-loathing. She pitied or despised blacks and the "blackness" in herself; she hated or feared whites yet desperately sought their approval. In a race-based society, the tragic mulatto found peace only in death. She evoked pity or scorn, not sympathy.

Vera Caspary's novel *The White Girl* told the story of Solaria, a beautiful multiracial woman who passes for white. Her secret is revealed by the appearance of her brown-skinned brother. Depressed, and believing that her skin is becoming darker, Solaria drinks poison. A more realistic

but equally depressing mulatto character is found in Geoffrey Barnes's novel *Dark Lustre*. Alpine, the light-skinned "heroine," dies in childbirth, but her white baby lives to continue "a cycle of pain." Both Solaria and Alpine are repulsed by blacks, especially black suitors.[3]

The troubled mulatto is portrayed as a selfish woman who will give up all, including her black family, in order to live as a white person. These words are illustrative: "Don't come for me. If you see me in the street, don't speak to me. From this moment on I'm White. I am not colored. You have to give me up."

These words were spoken by Peola, a tortured, self-hating black girl in the 1934 movie *Imitation of Life*.[4] Peola, played adeptly by Fredi Washington, had skin that was white. But she was not socially white. She was multiracial. Peola was tired of being treated as a second-class citizen; tired, that is, of being treated like a 1930s black American. She passed for white and begged her mother to understand.

Peola is the antithesis of the mammy caricature. Delilah knows her place in the Jim Crow hierarchy: the bottom rung. Hers is an accommodating resignation, bordering on contentment. Peola hates her life, wants more, wants to live as a white person, to have the opportunities that whites enjoy. Delilah hopes that her daughter will accept her racial heritage. "He [God] made you black, honey. Don't be telling Him His business. Accept it, honey." Peola wants to be loved by a white man, to marry a white man. She is beautiful, sensual, a potential wife to any white man who does not know her secret. Peola wants to live without the stigma of having a black ancestor—and in the 1930s that stigma was real and measurable. Ultimately and inevitably, Peola rejects her mother, runs away, and lives as a white person. Delilah dies of a broken heart. A repentant and tearful Peola returns to her mother's funeral.

Audiences, black and white (and they were separate), hated what Peola did to her mother—and they hated Peola. She is often portrayed as the epitome of selfishness. In many academic discussions about tragic mulattoes the name Peola is included. From the mid-1930s through the late 1970s, Peola was an epithet used by blacks against light-skinned black women who identified with mainstream white society. A Peola looked white and wanted to be white. During the civil rights movement and the black power movement, the name Peola was an insult comparable to Uncle Tom, albeit a light-skinned female version.

Fredi Washington, the black actress who played Peola, was multiracial with skin light enough to pass for white. Rumor has it that in later movies makeup was used to blacken her skin so white audiences would know her race. She had sharply defined features—long, dark, and straight hair, and green eyes—that limited the roles she was offered. She could

Section of the museum with tragic mulatto objects.

not play mammy roles, and though she looked white, no acknowledged black was allowed to play a white person.

Imitation of Life was remade in 1959.[5] The plot is essentially the same, but Peola is called Sara Jane and is played by Susan Kohner, a white actress. Delilah is now Annie Johnson. The pancake storyline is gone. Instead, the white mistress is a struggling actress. The crux of the story remains the light-skinned girl's attempts to pass for white. She runs away and becomes a chorus girl in a sleazy nightclub. Her dark-skinned mother (played by Juanita Moore) follows her. She begs her mother to leave her alone. Sara Jane does not want to marry a "colored chauffeur"; she wants a white boyfriend. She gets a white boyfriend, but when he discovers her secret, he savagely beats her and leaves her in a gutter. As in the original, Sara Jane's mother dies from a broken heart, and the repentant child tearfully returns to the funeral.

Peola and Sara Jane were cinematic tragic mulattoes. They were big screen testaments to the commonly held belief that "mixed blood" brought sorrow. If only they did not have a "drop of Negro blood." Many audience members nodded agreement when Annie Johnson asked rhetorically, "How do you explain to your daughter that she was born to hurt?"

Were real mulattoes born to hurt? All racial minorities in the United States have been victimized by the dominant group, although the expressions of that oppression vary. Mulattoes were considered black; therefore, they were slaves along with their darker kinsmen. All slaves were "born to hurt," but some writers have argued that mulattoes were privileged, relative to dark-skinned blacks. E.B. Reuter, a historian, wrote:

> In slavery days, they were most frequently the trained servants and had the advantages of daily contact with cultured men and women. Many of them were free and so enjoyed whatever advantages went with that superior status. They were considered by the white people to be superior in intelligence to the black Negroes, and came to take great pride in the fact of their white blood. . . . When possible, they formed a sort of mixed-blood caste and held themselves aloof from the black Negroes and the slaves of lower status.[6]

Reuter's claim that mulattoes were held in higher regard and treated better than "pure blacks" must be examined closely. American slavery lasted for more than two centuries; therefore, it is difficult to generalize about the institution. The interactions between slaveholder and slaves varied across decades and from plantation to plantation. Nevertheless, there are clues regarding the status of mulattoes. In a variety of public statements and laws, the offspring of white-black sexual relations were referred to as "mongrels" or "spurious."[7] Also, these interracial children were legally defined as pure blacks, which was different from how they were handled in other New World countries. A slaveholder claimed that there was "not an old plantation in which the grandchildren of the owner [therefore mulattoes] are not whipped in the field by his overseer."[8] Further, it seems that mulatto women were sometimes targeted for sexual abuse.

According to the historian J.C. Furnas, in some slave markets, mulattoes and quadroons brought higher prices, because of their use as sexual objects.[9] Some slavers found dark skin vulgar and repulsive. The mulatto approximated the white ideal of female attractiveness. All slave women (and men and children) were vulnerable to being raped, but the mulatto afforded the slave owner the opportunity to rape, with impunity, a woman who was physically white (or near-white) but legally black. A greater likelihood of being raped is certainly not an indication of favored status.

The mulatto woman was depicted as a seductress whose beauty drove white men to rape her. This is an obvious and flawed attempt to reconcile the prohibitions against miscegenation (interracial sexual relations) with the reality that whites routinely used blacks as sexual objects. One slaver noted, "There is not a likely looking girl in this State that is not the concubine of a White man."[10] Every mulatto was proof that the color line had been crossed. In this regard, mulattoes were symbols of rape and concubinage. Historian Gary B. Nash summarized the slavery-era relationship between the rape of black women, the handling of mulattoes, and white dominance:

> Though skin color came to assume importance through generations of association with slavery, white colonists developed few qualms about intimate contact with black women. But raising the social status of those who labored at the bottom of society and who were defined as abysmally inferior was a matter of serious concern. It was resolved by insuring that the mulatto would not occupy a position midway between white and black. Any black blood classified a person as black; and to be black was to be a slave. . . . By prohibiting racial intermarriage, winking at interracial sex, and defining all mixed offspring as black, white society found the ideal answer to its labor needs, its extracurricular and inadmissible sexual desires, its compulsion to maintain its culture purebred, and the problem of maintaining, at least in theory, absolute social control.[11]

George M. Frederickson, author of *The Black Image in the White Mind*, claimed that many white Americans believed that mulattoes were a degenerate race because they had "white blood," which made them ambitious and power hungry, combined with "black blood," which made them animalistic and savage. The attributing of personality and morality traits to "blood" seems foolish today, but it was taken seriously in the past. Fredrickson singles out Charles Carroll, author of *The Negro a Beast*, who described blacks as apelike.[12] Carroll said that mulattoes were the offspring of "unnatural relationships" and did not have "the right to live" because when they grew up they became rapists and killers.[13] His claim was untrue but widely believed. In 1899 a southern white woman, L.H. Harris, wrote to the editor of the *Independent* that the "negro brute" who rapes white women was "nearly always a mulatto," with "enough white blood in him to replace native humility and cowardice with Caucasian audacity."[14] Mulatto women were depicted as emotionally troubled seducers and mulatto men as power-hungry criminals.

In Nella Larsen's novel *Passing*, Clare, a mulatto passing for white, frequently is drawn to blacks in Harlem. Her bigoted white husband finds her there. Her problems are solved when she falls to her death from a sixth-story window. In the 1936 movie *Show Boat*, a beautiful young entertainer, Julie, discovers that she has "Negro blood." Existing laws held that "one drop of Negro blood makes you a Negro." Her husband (and the movie's writers and producer) take this "one-drop rule" literally. The husband cuts her hand with a knife and sucks her blood. This supposedly makes him a Negro. Afterward Julie and her newly mulattoed husband walk hand-in-hand. Nevertheless, she is a screen mulatto, so the movie ends with this once cheerful "white" woman as a Negro alcoholic.[15]

Lost Boundaries is a book by William L. White, made into a movie in 1949.[16] It tells the story of a troubled mulatto couple, the Johnsons. The husband is a physician, but he cannot get a job in a southern black hospital because he "looks white," and no southern white hospital will hire him. The Johnsons move to New England and pass for white. They become pillars of their local community—all the while terrified of being discredited. Years later, when their secret is discovered, the townspeople turn against them. The town's white minister delivers a sermon on racial tolerance which leads the locals, shamefaced and guilt-ridden, to befriend again the mulatto couple. *Lost Boundaries*, despite the white minister's sermon, blames the mulatto couple, not a racist culture, for the discrimination and personal conflicts faced by the Johnsons.

In 1958 Natalie Wood starred in *Kings Go Forth*, the story of a young French mulatto who passes for white.[17] She becomes involved with two American soldiers on leave from World War II. They are both infatuated with her until they discover that her father is black. Both men desert her. She attempts suicide unsuccessfully. Given another chance to live, she

Grotesque image of black woman from unknown book. This is the image that Henry Louis Gates Jr. found the most disturbing in the museum.

Skin brighteners, like this product made in 1946, were popular during the Jim Crow period in the United States. Today, they are popular in many countries.

turns her family's large home into a hostel for war orphans, "those just as deprived of love as herself."[18] At the movie's end, one of the soldiers is dead; the other, missing an arm, returns to the mulatto woman. They are comparable, both damaged, and it is implied that they will marry.

The mulatto women in *Show Boat*, *Lost Boundaries*, and *Kings Go Forth* were portrayed by white actresses. It was a common practice. Producers felt that white audiences would feel sympathy for a tortured white woman, even if she was portraying a mulatto character. The audience knew she was really white. In *Pinky*, Jeanne Crain, a well-known actress, played the role of the troubled mulatto.[19] Her dark-skinned grandmother was played by Ethel Waters. When audiences saw Ethel Waters doing menial labor, it was consistent with their understanding of a mammy's life, but when Jeanne Crain was shown washing other people's clothes, audiences cried.

Even black filmmakers like Oscar Micheaux made movies with tragic mulattoes. *Within Our Gates* tells the story of a mulatto woman who is hit by a car, menaced by a con man, nearly raped by a white man, and witnesses the lynching of her entire family. *God's Step Children* tells the story of Naomi, a mulatto who leaves her black husband and child and passes for white. Later, consumed by guilt, she commits suicide. Multiracial actresses played these roles.[20]

Fredi Washington, in *Imitation of Life*, was one of the first cinematic tragic mulattoes. She was followed by women like Dorothy Dandridge and Nina Mae McKinney. Dandridge deserves special attention because she not only portrayed doomed, unfulfilled women, but she was the embodiment of the tragic mulatto in real life. Her role as the lead character in *Carmen Jones* helped make her a star. She was the first black woman featured on the cover of *Life* magazine. In *Island in the Sun* she was the first black woman to be held—lovingly—in the arms of a white man in an American movie.[21] She was a beautiful and talented actress, but Hollywood was not ready for a black leading lady; the only roles offered to her were variants of the tragic mulatto theme. Her personal life was filled with failed relationships. Disillusioned by roles that limited her to exotic, self-destructive mulatto types, she went to Europe, where she fared worse. She died in 1965, at the age of forty-two, from an overdose of antidepressants.

Today's successful multiracial actresses—for example, Halle Berry, Beyoncé, Mariah Carey, and Kidada Jones—owe a debt to the pioneering efforts of Dandridge. These women have great wealth and fame. They are biracial, but their statuses and circumstances are not tragic. They are not marginalized; they are mainstream celebrities. Dark-skinned actresses Whoopi Goldberg, Angela Bassett, Alfre Woodard, and Joie Lee have enjoyed comparable success. They, too, benefit from Dandridge's path clearing.

The tragic mulatto was more myth than reality; Dandridge was an exception. The mulatto was made tragic in the minds of whites who reasoned that the greatest tragedy was to be near-white: so close, yet a racial gulf away. The near-white was to be pitied—and shunned. There were undoubtedly light-skinned blacks, male and female, who felt marginalized in this race-conscious culture. This was true for many people of color, including dark-skinned blacks. Self-hatred and intraracial hatred are not limited to light-skinned blacks. There is evidence that all racial minorities in the United States have battled feelings of inferiority and in-group animosity; those are, unfortunately, the costs of being a minority.

The tragic mulatto stereotype claims that mulattoes occupy the margins of two worlds, fitting into neither, accepted by neither. This is not true of real-life mulattoes. Historically, mulattoes were not only accepted into the black community, but were often its leaders and spokespersons, both nationally and at neighborhood levels. Frederick Douglass, W.E.B.

Du Bois, Booker T. Washington, Elizabeth Ross Hayes,[22] Mary Church Terrell,[23] Thurgood Marshall, Malcolm X, and Louis Farrakhan were all multiracial. Walter White, the former head of the NAACP, and Adam Clayton Powell, an outspoken congressman, were both light enough to pass for white. Other notable mulattoes include Langston Hughes, Billie Holiday, and the writer Jean Toomer, who was the grandson of mulatto Reconstruction politician P.B.S. Pinchback.

There was tragedy in the lives of light-skinned black women, but there was also tragedy in the lives of most dark-skinned black women—and men and children. The tragedy was not that they were black, or had a drop of "Negro blood," although whites saw that as a tragedy. Rather, the real tragedy was the way race was used to limit the chances of people of color. The twenty-first century finds an America increasingly more tolerant of interracial unions and the resulting offspring.

In the twenty-first century the concept of women as tragic mulattoes is antiquated and offensive. This development is, in part, a result of the general societal acceptance of interracial dating and marriages. A Pew Research report that used census data showed that almost 15 percent of all new marriages in the United States in 2010 were between spouses of a different race or ethnicity from one another, more than double the share in 1980 (6.7 percent). Among all newlyweds in 2010, 9 percent of whites, 17 percent of blacks, 26 percent of Hispanics and 28 percent of Asians married someone of a different race.[24] The United States society is more accepting of interracial marriages and more accepting of the children produced by these relationships.

Preying on Black Women

The portrayal of black women as lascivious by nature is an enduring stereotype. The descriptive words associated with this stereotype are singular in their focus: seductive, alluring, worldly, beguiling, tempting, and lewd. Historically, white women, as a category, were portrayed as models of self-respect, self-control, and modesty—even sexual purity—but black women were often portrayed as innately promiscuous, even predatory. This depiction of black women is signified by the name Jezebel.[25]

Sue Jewell, a contemporary sociologist, conceptualized the Jezebel as a tragic mulatto—"thin lips, long straight hair, slender nose, thin figure and fair complexion."[26] This conceptualization is too narrow. It is true that the so-called tragic mulatto and Jezebel share the reputation of being sexually seductive, and both are antithetical to the desexualized mammy caricature; nevertheless, it is a mistake to assume that only, or even mainly, fair-complexioned black women were sexually objectified by the larger American society. From the early 1630s to the present,

Small planter souvenir object (circa 1930s).

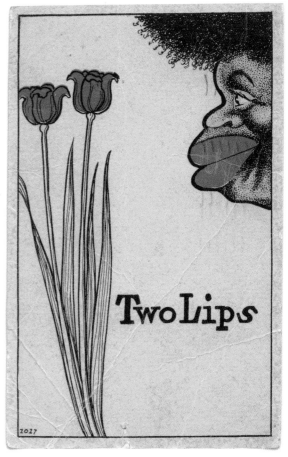

black American women of all shades have been portrayed as hypersexual "bad-black-girls."[27]

Jewell's conceptualization is based on a kernel of historical truth. Many of the slavery-era blacks sold into prostitution were mulattoes. Also, freeborn light-skinned black women sometimes became the concubines of wealthy white southerners. This system, called placage, involved a formal arrangement for the white suitor/customer to financially support the black woman and her children in exchange for her long-term sexual services. The white men often met the black women at "Quadroon Balls," a genteel sex market.

The belief that blacks are sexually lewd predates the institution of slavery in America. European travelers to Africa found scantily clad natives. This seminudity was misinterpreted as lewdness. White Europeans, locked into the racial ethnocentrism of the seventeenth century, saw African polygamy and tribal dances as proof of the African's uncontrolled sexual lust. Europeans were fascinated by African sexuality. William Bosman described the black women on the coast of Guinea as "fiery" and "warm" and "so much hotter than the men."[28] William Smith described African women as "hot constitution'd Ladies" who "are continually contriving stratagems how to gain a lover."[29] The genesis of anti-black sexual archetypes emerged from the writings of these and other Europeans: the black male as brute and potential rapist; the black woman as Jezebel whore.

The English colonists accepted the Elizabethan image of "the lusty Moor," and used this and similar stereotypes to justify enslaving blacks. In part, this was accomplished by arguing that blacks were subhumans: intellectually inferior, culturally stunted, morally underdeveloped, and animal-like sexually. Whites used racist and sexist ideologies to argue that they alone were civilized and rational, whereas blacks, and other people of color, were barbaric and deserved to be subjugated.[30]

The Jezebel stereotype was used during slavery as a rationalization for sexual relations between white men and black women, especially sexual unions involving slavers and slaves. The Jezebel was depicted as a black woman with an insatiable appetite for sex. She was not satisfied with black men. The slavery-era Jezebel, it was claimed, desired sexual relations with white men; therefore, white men did not have to rape black women. James Redpath, an abolitionist no less, wrote that slave women were "gratified by the criminal advances of Saxons."[31] This view is contradicted by Frederick Douglass, the abolitionist and former slave, who claimed that the "slave woman is at the mercy of the fathers, sons or brothers of her master."[32] Douglass's account is consistent with the accounts of other former slaves. Henry Bibb's master forced a young slave

TOP: Lucky Brown Pressing Oil, 1936.
BOTTOM LEFT: Bar set, 1950s.
BOTTOM RIGHT: Postcard, postmarked 1909.

to be his son's concubine; later, Bibb and his wife were sold to a Kentucky trader who forced Bibb's wife into prostitution.[33]

Slave women were property; therefore, legally they could not be raped. Often slavers would offer gifts or promises of reduced labor if the slave women would consent to sexual relations, and there were instances of the slaver and slave sharing sexual attraction, but "the rape of a female slave was probably the most common form of interracial sex."[34] A Georgia slave woman explained, "When he make me follow him into de bush, what use me to tell him no? He have strength to make me."[35] At the same time, black men convicted of raping white women were usually castrated, hanged, or both.[36]

People make decisions based on the options they have and the options that they perceive. The objective realities of slavery and the slaves' subjective interpretations of the institution both led female slaves to engage "voluntarily" in sexual unions with whites, especially slavers and their sons, and overseers. A slave who refused the sexual advances of her slaver risked being sold, beaten, raped, and having her "husband" or children sold. Many slave women conceded to sexual relations with whites, thereby reinforcing the belief that black women were lustful and available.

The idea that black women were naturally and inevitably sexually promiscuous was reinforced by several features of the slavery institution. Slaves, whether on the auction block or offered privately for sale, were often stripped naked and physically examined. In theory, this was done to insure that they were healthy, able to reproduce, and, equally important, to look for whipping scars—the presence of which implied that the slave was rebellious. In practice, the stripping and touching of slaves had a sexually exploitative, sometimes sadistic function.[37] Nakedness, especially among women in the eighteenth and nineteenth centuries, implied lack of civility, morality, and sexual restraint even when the nakedness was forced. Slaves, of both sexes and all ages, often wore few clothes or clothes so ragged that their legs, thighs, and chests were exposed. Conversely, whites, especially women, wore clothing over most of their bodies. The contrast between the clothing reinforced the beliefs that white women were civilized, modest, and sexually pure, whereas black women were uncivilized, immodest, and sexually aberrant.

Black slave women were also frequently pregnant. The institution of slavery depended on black women to supply future slaves. By every method imaginable, slave women were "encouraged" to reproduce. Some slavers, for example, offered a new pig for each child born to a slave family, a new dress to the slave woman for each surviving infant, or no work on Saturdays to black women who produced six children.[38] Young

This 1950s fishing lure demonstrates that racist imagery was common with everyday objects.

black girls were encouraged to have sex as "anticipatory socialization" for their later status as "breeders." When they did reproduce, their fecundity was seen as proof of their insatiable sexual appetites. Deborah Gray White, a historian, wrote:

> Major periodicals carried articles detailing optimal conditions under which bonded women were known to reproduce, and the merits of a particular "breeder" were often the topic of parlor or dinner table conversations. The fact that something so personal and private became a matter of public discussion prompted one ex-slave to declare that "women wasn't nothing but cattle." Once reproduction became a topic of public conversation, so did the slave woman's sexual activities.[39]

The Jezebel stereotype is contradicted by several historical facts. Although black women, especially those with brown or tan skin and "European features," were sometimes forced into prostitution for white men, "slaves had no prostitution and very little venereal disease within their communities."[40] Slaves rarely chose spouses from among their blood relatives. Slavers often encouraged, and sometimes mandated, sexual promiscuity among their slaves; nevertheless, most slaves sought long-term, monogamous relationships. Slaves "married" when allowed, and adultery was frowned upon in most black "communities." During Reconstruction "slaves eagerly legitimated their unions, holding mass-marriage ceremonies and individual weddings."[41]

Unfortunately for black women, Emancipation and Reconstruction did not stop their sexual victimization. To again quote White, "From emancipation through more than two-thirds of the twentieth century, no Southern white male was convicted of raping or attempting to rape a black woman. Yet the crime was widespread." Black women, especially in the South or border states, had virtually no legal recourse when raped by white men, and many were reluctant to report their victimization by black men, fearing that the men would be lynched.[42]

Jezebel in the Twentieth Century

The portrayal of black women as Jezebel whores began in slavery, extended through the Jim Crow period, and continues today. Although the mammy caricature was the dominant popular cultural image of black women from slavery to the 1950s, the depiction of black women as Jezebels was common in American material culture. Everyday items—such as ashtrays, postcards, sheet music, fishing lures, drinking glasses, and so forth—depicted naked or scantily dressed black women, lacking modesty and sexual restraint. For example, a metal nutcracker (circa

1930s) depicts a topless Black woman. The nut is placed under her skirt, in her crotch, and crushed.[43] Items like this one reflected and shaped white attitudes toward black female sexuality. An analysis of the Jezebel images in the Jim Crow Museum of Racist Memorabilia reveals several patterns.

Many of the Jezebel objects caricature and mock African women. For example, in the 1950s "ZULU-LULU" was a popular set of swizzle sticks used for stirring drinks. There were several versions of this product but all show silhouettes of naked African women of various ages. One version read: "Nifty at 15, spiffy at 20, sizzling at 25, perky at 30, declining at 35, droopy at 40." There were versions that included depictions of African women at fifty and sixty years of age. ZULU-LULU was billed as a party gag as illustrated by this advertisement on the product: "Don't pity Lulu— you're not getting younger yourself . . . laugh with your guests when they find these hilarious swizzle sticks in their drinks. ZULU-LULU will be the most popular girl at your party."

The Jezebel images which defame African women may be viewed in two broad categories: pathetic others and exotic others. Pathetic others include those depictions of African women as physically unattractive,

Ceramic piece sold in the 1950s.

unintelligent, and uncivilized. These images suggest that African women in particular and black women in general possess aberrant physical, social, and cultural traits. The African woman's features are distorted—her lips are exaggerated, her breasts sag, she is often inebriated. The pathetic other, like the mammy caricature before her, is drawn to refute the claim that white men find black women sexually appealing. Yet this depiction of the African woman has an obvious sexual component: she is often placed in a sexual setting, naked or near naked, inebriated or holding a drink, her eyes suggesting a sexual longing. She is a sexual being, but not one that white men would consider.

An example of the pathetic other is a banner (circa 1930s) showing a drunken African woman with the caption, "Martini Anyone?"[44] The message is clear: this pathetic other is too ugly, too stupid, and too different to elicit sexual attraction from reasonable men; instead, she is a source of pity, laughter, and derision.

It must be emphasized that the items that depict African and African American women as one-dimensional sexual beings are often everyday items—found in the homes, garages, automobiles, and offices of "mainstream" Americans. These items are functional—in addition to promoting antiblack stereotypes, they also have practical utility. For example, a topless bust of a black woman with a fishing hook attached functions as an object of racial stereotyping and as a fishing lure. One such object was the "Virgin Fishing Lucky Lure" (circa 1950s). It has become a highly sought after collectible nationwide.

An analysis of Jezebel images also reveals that black female children are sexually objectified. Black girls, with the faces of preteenagers, are drawn with adult-sized buttocks, which are exposed. They are naked, scantily clad, or hiding seductively behind towels, blankets, trees, or other objects. A 1949 postcard shows a naked black girl hiding her genitals with a paper fan. Although she has the appearance of a small child she has noticeable breasts. The accompanying caption reads: "Honey, I'se Waitin' Fo' You Down South."[45] The sexual innuendo is obvious.

Another postcard (circa 1950s) shows a black girl, approximately eight years old, standing in a watermelon patch. She has a protruding stomach. The caption reads: "Oh—I is Not! . . . It Must Be Sumthin' I Et!!" Her exposed right shoulder and the churlish grin suggest that the protruding stomach resulted from a sexual experience, not overeating. The portrayal of this prepubescent girl as pregnant suggests that black females are sexually active and sexually irresponsible even as small children.

The belief that black women are sexually promiscuous is propagated by innumerable images of pregnant black women and black women with large numbers of children. A 1947 greeting card depicting a black mammy bears the caption: "Ah keeps right on sendin' em!" Inside is a young black woman with eight small children. The inside caption reads: "As long as you keeps on havin' em."

In the 1964 presidential election between Lyndon Johnson and Barry Goldwater, Johnson used the political slogan, "All the way with L.B.J." A mid-1960s license plate shows a caricatured black woman, pregnant, with these words, "I went all de way wif L.B.J." Johnson received overwhelming support from black voters. The image on the license plate, which also appeared on posters and smaller prints, insults blacks generally, black Democrats, and black women.

Black Jezebels in American Cinema

In the 1915 movie *The Birth of a Nation*, Lydia Brown is a mulatto character.[46] She is the mistress of the white character Senator Stoneman. Lydia is savage, corrupt, and lascivious. She is portrayed as overtly sexual, and she uses her "feminine wiles" to deceive the formerly good white man. Lydia's characterization was rare in early American cinema. There was a scattering of black "loose women" and "fallen women" on the big screen, but it would be another half century before the depiction of cinematic black women as sexually promiscuous would become commonplace.

By the 1970s black moviegoers had tired of cinematic portrayals of blacks as mammies, Toms, tragic mulattoes, and picaninnies. In the 1970s blacks willingly, though unwittingly, exchanged the old negative caricatures for new ones. These new caricatures were popularized by the two hundred mostly B-grade films now labeled blaxploitation movies.

These movies supposedly depicted realistic black experiences, but many were produced and directed by whites. Daniel J. Leab, the movie historian, noted, "Whites packaged, financed, and sold these films, and they received the bulk of the big money."[47] The world depicted in blaxploitation movies included corrupt police and politicians, pimps, drug dealers, violent criminals, and prostitutes. In the main, these movies were low-budget, formulaic interpretations of black life by white producers, directors, and distributors. Black actors and actresses, many unable to find work in mainstream movies, found work in blaxploitation movies. Black patrons supported these movies because they showed blacks fighting the "white establishment," resisting police corruption, acting assertively, and having sex lives.

The film which ushered in the blaxploitation period was *Sweet Sweetback's Baadasssss Song*, written, directed, produced, and starred in by Melvin Van Peebles.[48] The story centers on Sweet, an amoral and hedonistic hustler and pimp, who kills two white cops who were attacking a young black radical. He spends the rest of the movie on the lam,

113

114

running from racist cops and to pimps, gangsters, bikers, and whores. Sweet's "revolutionary consciousness" is heightened because of his first-hand experience with police corruption, and by the movie's end he has become a heroic, almost mythical, black revolutionary. The film ends with the message: "A BAADASSSSS NIGGER IS COMING BACK TO COLLECT SOME DUES."

Sweet Sweetback's Baadasssss Song was originally rated X. After decades of asexual and desexualized black Tom characters, black audiences were ready for a sexually assertive black male movie character. Sweet was reared in a brothel. In one flashback scene, a ten-year-old Sweet (played by Van Peebles's real-life son Mario) is graphically taught how to make love by an older prostitute. Sweetback is slang for "large penis" and "great lovemaking ability." Much of the movie centers on Sweet's lovemaking abilities, and this movie helped promote the "black sex machine" characterization of black men common in later movies. *Sweet Sweetback's Baadasssss Song* also gave impetus to cinematic portrayals of black women as Jezebel whores. According to Donald Bogle:

> With the glamorization of the ghetto, however, came also the elevation of the Pimp/outlaw/rebel as folk hero. Van Peebles played up this new sensibility, and his film was the first to glorify the pimp. It failed, however, to explain the social conditions that made the pimp such an important figure. At the same time, the movie debased the black woman, depicting her as little more than a whore.[49]

The commercial success of *Sweet Sweetback's Baadasssss Song* inspired many imitators. A formula for these "black action" movies emerged: a justifiably angry black male seeks revenge on corrupt white police officers, politicians, or drug dealers. In the process of extracting revenge his political consciousness is raised and he has numerous sexual exploits. Van Peebles, a black man, aided in creating this formula, and it served as the template for the whites who wrote, directed, and produced blaxploitation movies.

The movies that followed *Sweet Sweetback's Baadasssss Song* increasingly limited black actresses to Jezebel-type roles. Lynn Hamilton, a black actress, auditioned for the role of a "strong Angela Davis type." At the beginning of the audition she was asked if she would play nude scenes. She said of the role and character: "Here is this woman who holds all kinds of academic degrees and has a high position opening the door totally nude to admit her boyfriend, a policeman. The first thing he says is, 'Fix me some breakfast.'"[50] She fries bacon, grease splattering, while her boyfriend fondles her breasts and buttocks.

This postcard was copyrighted in 1906 by White City Art Company.

Many black women in these blaxploitation movies functioned as sexual fodder, legitimizing the street credentials of the black male super-hero. Even when black women were the central characters of the movies, they were still portrayed as sexually aggressive, often deviants. Black actresses such as Pam Grier and Tamara Dobson built their acting careers starring in blaxploitation movies. Their characters resembled those of the male superheroes: they were physically attractive and aggressive rebels, willing and able to gain revenge against corrupt officials, drug dealers, and violent criminals. According to Donald Bogle:

> Like the old-style mammies, they ran not simply a household but a universe unto itself. Often they were out to clean up the ghetto of drug pushers, protecting the black hearth and home from corrupt infiltrators. Dobson and Grier represented Woman as Protector, Nurturer, Communal Mother Surrogate. Yet, these women also had the look and manner of old-style mulattoes. They were often perceived as being exotic sex objects (Grier's raw sexuality was always exploited)—yet with a twist. Although men manhandle them, Grier and Dobson also took liberties with men, at times using them as playful, comic toys.[51]

The portrayal of black women as sexually lascivious became commonplace in American movies. Grier, for example, in *Coffy* and *Foxy Brown* goes undercover as a "whore" to get revenge on whites who have victimized her loved ones. In *The Big Bird Cage*, Carol Speed plays a spunky black hooker inmate. The 1973 movie *Black Hooker* (a.k.a. *Street Sisters*) is a movie about a white-skin boy whose mother is an uncaring black whore. In the made-for-television movie, *Dummy*, Irma Riley plays a black prostitute. Lisa Bonet, one of the daughters on *The Cosby Show*, plays a voodoo priestess in *Angel Heart*. Her character, Epiphany Proudfoot, has a sexual episode with Harry Angel (Mickey Rourke) that was so graphic that the movie almost received an X rating. In *Harlem Nights*, Sunshine (played by Lela Rochon) is a prostitute so skilled that a white lover calls his wife on the telephone to tell her that he is never returning home.[52]

The obligatory "black whore" is added to urban-themed movies, apparently to give "real life" authenticity. In the classic movie *Taxi Driver*, a black hooker (Copper Cunningham) has sex with a white business-man in the backseat of the taxi driven by Travis Bickle (Robert De Niro). The sex act is offered as evidence of the moral decline and decadence of America. Bickle washes his taxi after the sex act. Hazelle Goodman plays Cookie, a hooker in Woody Allen's *Deconstructing Harry*. When Cookie is asked if she knows what a black hole is, she replies, "what I make my living with." In the credits listed for *Dangerous Ground*, Temsie Times is listed as "Black Hooker." Cathy Tyson, the niece of actress Cicely Tyson, got her first major role as a sophisticated call girl in *Mona Lisa*. The racial and sexual stereotypes depicted in these and similar movies find their fuller, clearer expression in low-budget pornographic movies.[53]

The pornography industry remains a bastion of explicit antiblack stereotyping—raw, obscene, and increasing mainstream. While most of the heterosexual-themed movies in the American pornographic market have white actresses, there are hundreds of pornographic movies that also depict black women as "sexual things"—and as "sexual animals." Internet stores sell videos with titles like *Black Chicks in Heat*, *Black Bitches*, *Hoochie Mamas*, *Video Sto' Ho*, *Black and Nasty*, *South Central Hookers*, and *Git Yo' Ass on Da Bus!* In the privacy of their homes or hotel rooms, Americans can watch black actresses—Purple Passion, Jamaica, Toy, Chocolate Tye, Juicy, Jazz, Spontaneeus Xtasy, and others—"validate" the belief that black women are whores. Most of the black actresses in mainstream movies who play Jezebel roles, especially those with inter-racial sex scenes, are light-skinned or brown-skinned women, but most black women in pornographic movies are brown-skinned and dark-skinned women.

Halle Berry won an academy award for the role of Leticia Musgrove in *Monster's Ball*, a complex and haunting drama.[54] Leticia had a sexual relationship with Hank Grotowski (Billy Bob Thornton), a racist jailer who supervised the execution of her husband. The link between Leticia's black husband's execution and her white lover was not revealed to her until the movie's end, by then she and Hank were bonded together—self-loathers, angry, defeated, drunk, grieving the loss of relatives, trying frantically to find redemption, and failing that, someone to share the emotional pain. Their initial sexual encounter followed a drunken lamentation of their failures as parents. She lost her husband, and then her son was killed. His son committed suicide, in his presence. Writhing in emotional pain, she begged, "Make me feel better." There followed one of the rawest, most intense sexual scenes in American cinematic history. Later, he gave her a truck. He named his new business venture, a service station, Leticia. He readied a room in his home, moved his racist father to a convalescent home, and after Leticia was evicted from her home he moved her into his house.

The relationship between Hank and Leticia was an updated version of the placage arrangements common in the 1800s. The first night after she moved into his home they lie in bed. He said, "I'm gonna take care of you." Leticia replied, "Good, 'cause I really need to be taken care of." In a tender moment, he went to a store to get ice cream. While he was gone

she found evidence that he was involved in her husband's execution. She cried, wailed, gripped with gut-wrenching pain. He returned. She had a dazed look. He told her, "You look real pretty. Let's go out on the steps, if you want to." She followed him. Outside, she accepted a spoon, stared at his son's tombstone, and then accepted ice cream from his spoon. His last words were, "I think we gonna be alright." Angela Bassett, who was nominated for an Academy Award for her portrayal of Tina Turner in *What's Love Got to Do with It*, rejected the role of Leticia. In an interview with *Newsweek*, she said: "It's about character, darling. I wasn't going to be a prostitute on film. I couldn't do that because it's such a stereotype about black women and sexuality."[55] Bassett's assessment was harsh and probably overstated. Leticia was portrayed as a "loose woman": drinking from a bottle, slouched, legs open, later initiating sex with a man she barely knew. She ended the movie as a "kept woman," not a prostitute—her status is a function of the harsh realities of being a poor, black woman in a society that devalues the poor, the black, and women. Bassett insisted that she was not criticizing Berry so much as the Hollywood system for continuing to typecast black women in demeaning roles. This was a reasonable criticism. Only a handful of black actresses and actors have won Academy Awards, and most won because they brought depth and complexity to otherwise one-dimensional stereotypical roles: Hattie McDaniel played a mammy in *Gone with the Wind*; Sidney Poitier played a Tom, albeit a dignified one, in *Lilies of the Field*; and Denzel Washington was a rogue cop, a variant of the Brute, in *Training Day*.[56]

The Jezebel has replaced the mammy as the dominant image of black women in American popular culture. The black woman as prostitute, for example, is a staple in mainstream movies, especially those with urban settings. The black prostitute and the black pimp supposedly give these movies cutting-edge realism. Small-budget pornographic movies reinforce vile sexual stereotypes of black women. These women are willing, sometimes predatory, sexual deviants who will fulfill any and all sexual fantasies. Their sexual performances tap into centuries-old images of black women as uninhibited whores. Music videos, especially those by gangsta rap performers, portray scantily clad, nubile black women who thrust their hips to lyrics which often depict them as 'hos, skeezers, and bitches. A half century after the American civil rights movement, it is increasingly easy to find black women, especially young ones, depicted as Jezebels whose only value is as sexual commodities.

Sapphire

The Sapphire caricature portrays black women as rude, loud, malicious, stubborn, and overbearing.[57] This is the Angry Black Woman (ABW)

Modern reproduction of skin-whitening bleach sold in the 1930s.

popularized in the cinema and on television. She is tart-tongued and emasculating, one hand on a hip and the other pointing and jabbing (or arms akimbo), violently and rhythmically rocking her head, mocking African American men for offenses ranging from being unemployed to sexually pursuing white women. She is a shrill nagger with irrational states of anger and indignation and is often mean-spirited and abusive. Although African American men are her primary targets, she has venom for anyone who insults or disrespects her. The Sapphire's desire to dominate and her hypersensitivity to injustices make her a perpetual complainer, but she does not criticize to improve things; rather, she criticizes because she is unendingly bitter and wishes that unhappiness on others. The Sapphire caricature is a harsh portrayal of African American women, but it is more than that; it is a social control mechanism that is employed to punish black women who violate the societal norms that encourage them to be passive, servile, nonthreatening, and unseen.

Sapphire Stevens

From the 1800s through the mid-1900s, black women were often portrayed in popular culture as "sassy mammies" who ran their own homes with iron fists, including berating black husbands and children. These women were allowed, at least symbolically, to defy some racial norms. During the Jim Crow period, when real blacks were often beaten, jailed, or killed for arguing with whites, fictional mammies were allowed to pretend-chastise whites, including men. Their sassiness was supposed to indicate that they were accepted as members of the white family, and acceptance of that sassiness implied that slavery and segregation were not overly oppressive. A well-known example of a sassy mammy was Hattie McDaniel, who played characters that were sassy and borderline impertinent, but always loyal. She was not a threat to the existing social order.[58]

It was not until the *Amos 'n' Andy* radio show that the characterization of African American women as domineering, aggressive, and emasculating shrews became popularly associated with the name Sapphire. The show was conceived by Freeman Gosden and Charles Correll, two white actors who portrayed the characters Amos Jones and Andy Brown by mimicking and mocking black behavior and dialect. At its best, *Amos 'n' Andy* was a situational comedy; at its worse, it was an auditory minstrel show.[59] The show, with a mostly white cast, aired on the radio from 1928 to 1960, with intermittent interruptions. The television version of the show, with network television's first all-black cast, aired on CBS from 1951 to 1953, with syndicated reruns from 1954 to 1966. It was removed, in large part, through the efforts of the National Association for the Advancement of Colored People and the civil rights movement. Both as a

This movie poster advertises a 1960 melodrama film that included a plotline involving interracial romance, a provocative topic for that time. **121**

radio show[60] and television show, *Amos 'n' Andy* was extremely popular, and this was unfortunate for African Americans because it popularized racial caricatures of blacks. Americans learned that blacks were comical, not as actors but as a race.

Amos 'n' Andy told stories about the everyday foibles of the members of the Mystic Knights of the Sea, a black fraternal lodge. The lead characters were Amos Jones, a Harlem taxi driver and his gullible friend, Andy Brown. Starring in a nontitle lead role was the character George "Kingfish" Stevens, the leader of the lodge. Many of the stories revolved around Kingfish, a get-rich-quick schemer and a con artist who avoided work, and, when possible, took financial advantage of the ignorance and naïveté of Andy and others.[61] Kingfish was the prototypical coon, a lazy, easily confused, chronically unemployed, financially inept buffoon given to malapropisms. Kingfish was married to Sapphire Stevens who regularly berated him as a failure. He represented the worst in racial stereotyping, and there was little redemptive about the character. His ignorance was highlighted by his nonsensical misuse of words, for example: "I deny the allegation, Your Honor, and I resents the alligator," and "I'se regusted." Kingfish was not a good thinker or speaker. Even worse, he was a crook without scruples. He was too lazy to work and not above exploiting his wife and friends.

In other words, he was a television embodiment of some of the unforgiving ideas that many Americans had about black men. Other characters, including Lightnin', a Stepin Fetchit–like character on the show, had jobs and were honest, but Kingfish's worthlessness justified Sapphire's harsh critique of his life. It must be noted that Sapphire Stevens directed her disgust at her husband; hers was not the generalized anger that is today associated with angry black women.

Later Sapphires in Situational Comedies

Sue Jewell opined that the Sapphire image necessitates the presence of an African American man; "It is the African American male that represents the point of contention, in an ongoing verbal dual between Sapphire and the African American male . . . [His] lack of integrity and use of cunning and trickery provides her with an opportunity to emasculate him through her use of verbal put downs."[62] In the all-black or mostly black situational comedies that have appeared on television from the 1970s to the present, the Sapphire is a stock character. Like Sapphire Stevens, she demeans and belittles lazy, ignorant, or otherwise flawed black male characters.

Blacks on television have been overrepresented in situational comedies and underrepresented in dramatic series; one problem with this imbalance is that blacks in situational comedies are portrayed in racially stereotypical ways in order to get laughs. Canned laughter prompts the

Postcard, postmarked 1910, showing angry black woman as Sapphire.

television audience to laugh as the angry black woman, the Sapphire, insults and mocks black males.

Aunt Esther (also called Aunt Anderson) was a Sapphire character on the television situational comedy *Sanford and Son*, which premiered on NBC in 1972, with a final episode in 1977, and is still running in syndication. She was the Bible-swinging, angry nemesis and sister-in-law of the main character, Fred. Theirs was a love-mostly-hate relationship. Fred would call Aunt Esther ugly and she would call him a "fish-eyed fool," an "old sucka," or a "beady-eyed heathen." Then, they would threaten to hit each other. Aunt Esther dominated her husband Woodrow, a mild-mannered alcoholic. In this latter relationship, you have the idea of the aggressive black woman dominating a weak, morally defective black man.

The situational comedy *Good Times* aired between 1974 and 1979 on the CBS television network. The show followed the life of the Evans family in a Chicago housing project modeled on the infamous Cabrini-Green projects. This was one of the first times that a poor family had been highlighted in a weekly television series. Episodes of *Good Times* dealt with the Evans's attempts to survive despite living in suffocating poverty. There were several racial caricatures on the show, most notably the son, James Evans Jr. (also called J.J.), who devolved into a coon-like minstrel. After the first season the episodes increasingly focused on J.J.'s stereotypically buffoonish behavior. Esther Rolle, who played the role of Florida Evans, the mother, expressed her dislike for J.J.'s character in a 1975 interview with *Ebony* magazine:

> He's eighteen and he doesn't work. He can't read or write. He doesn't think. The show didn't start out to be that . . . Little by little—with the help of the artist, I suppose, because they couldn't do that to me—they have made J.J. more stupid and enlarged the role. Negative images have been slipped in on us through the character of the oldest child.[63]

In black-themed situational comedies, when there is a coon character, there is often a Sapphire character to mock him. In *Good Times* a character that bantered with and mocked J.J. was his sister, Thelma. A clearer example of a Sapphire, however, was the neighbor, Willona Woods, though she rarely targeted J.J. Instead, Willona belittled Nathan Bookman, the overweight superintendent, and she put down a series of worthless boyfriends, an ex-husband, politicians, and other men with questionable morals and work ethics.

In situational comedies with a primarily black cast, the black male does not have to be lazy, thick-witted, or financially unsuccessful for him to be taunted by a Sapphire character. *The Jeffersons*, which aired from 1975 to 1985, focused on an upper-middle-class family that had climbed up from the working class—in the show's theme song there is the line, "We finally got a piece of the pie." George and Louise Jefferson were making so much money from their dry-cleaning businesses that they hired a housekeeper, Florence Johnston. Her relationship with George was often antagonistic and the back-talking, wisecracking housekeeper approximated a Sapphire. She often teased George about his short stature, balding head, and decisions.

Another example of a Sapphire was the character Pamela (Pam) James, who appeared on *Martin*, a situational comedy that aired from 1992 to 1997 on Fox. Pam was a badmouthed, wisecracking friend/foe of the lead character, Martin. Tichina Arnold, the actress who played Pam, plays Rochelle, a dominating, aggressive matriarch in the situational comedy *Everybody Hates Chris*, which ran from 2005 to 2009, and is still aired on cable television. Arnold has mastered the role of the angry, black woman.

Angry Black Women with Guns

The film genre called blaxploitation emerged in the early 1970s. These movies, which targeted urban black audiences, exchanged one set of racial caricatures—mammy, Tom, uncle, picaninny—for a new set of equally offensive racial caricatures—Bucks (sex-crazed deviants), Brutes, (pimps, hit-men, and dope peddlers), and Nats (Whites-haters). One old caricature, the Jezebel, was revamped. The portrayal of African American women as hypersexual temptresses was as old as American slavery, but during the blaxploitation period the Jezebel caricature and the Sapphire caricature merged into a hybrid: angry "whores" fighting injustice. Black actresses such as Pam Grier built careers starring in blaxploitation movies. Their characters resembled those of the black male superheroes: they were physically attractive and aggressive rebels, willing and able to use their bodies, brains, and guns to gain revenge against corrupt officials, drug dealers, and violent criminals. Their anger was not focused solely, or primarily, on black men but rather on injustice and the perpetuators of injustice.

In the film *Coffy*, Pam Grier plays a nurse by day and vigilante by night who conducts a brutal one-woman war on organized crime.[64] In the movie, she pretends to be a "strung-out whore" to get revenge on the drug dealers who got her little sister hooked on heroin. Coffy lures the culprits back to their room, where she graphically shoots one in the head and gives the other a fatal dose of heroin. The remainder of the movie finds Coffy using guns and her body to punish King George, a flamboyant pimp, the sadistic mobster Arturo Vitroni, and every mafioso and crooked cop who crosses her path.

A 1951 set of novelty cocktail mixers.

Sapphire in the Twenty-First Century

Today, the Sapphire is one of the dominant portrayals of black woman. This is evident in the words of Cal Thomas, a commentator for Fox News:

> Look at the image of angry black women on television. Politically you have Maxine Waters of California, liberal Democrat. She's always angry every time she gets on television. Cynthia McKinney, another angry black woman. And who are the black women you

see on the local news at night in cities all over the country. They're usually angry about something. They've had a son who has been shot in a drive-by shooting. They are angry at Bush. So you don't really have a profile of non-angry black women, of whom there are quite a few.[65]

Thomas, admittedly an untrained sociologist, expressed what many Americans see and internalize, namely, images of Sapphires: angry at black men, white men, white women, the federal government, racism, maybe life itself. Thomas, shortly after making his statements about black women, agreed with a co-panelist that Oprah Winfrey is not angry.

The portrayal of black women as angry Sapphires permeates this culture. A Google search of "Angry Black Women" or "ABW" will demonstrate how pervasive this caricature has become. She lives in most movies with an all-black or predominantly black cast. For example, there is Terri, cussing and insulting the "manhood" of black men in *Barbershop* and its sequel, *Barbershop 2*. There is the argumentative Angela in *Why Did I Get Married?* There are books devoted to angry black women, for example *The Angry Black Woman's Guide to Life*, and websites where you can buy Angry Black Bitch cups, shirts, pillows, tile coasters, aprons, mouse pads, and teddy bears. There is even a pseudo-malady called "Angry Black Woman Syndrome."[66]

The tabloid talk shows that became popular in the 1990s—*The Jerry Springer Show*, *The Jenny Jones Show*, *The Maury Povich Show*, and *The Ricki Lake Show*—helped reinforce the racial stereotypes of African Americans, including the stereotype of black women as angry, castrating shrews. By the early 2000s, the "trash talk" shows had receded in popularity, in part because of the emergence of so-called reality shows. Again, these shows served as vehicles for African American women to be portrayed as Sapphires. Vanessa E. Jones, from the *Boston Globe*, wrote of the Sapphire:

> You see elements of her in Alicia Calaway of "Survivor: All-Stars," who indulged in a temperamental bout of finger wagging during an argument in 2001's "Survivor: The Australian Outback." Coral Smith, who rules with an iron tongue on MTV's "Real World/Road Rules Challenge: The Inferno," browbeat one female cast mate so badly a week ago that she challenged Smith to a fight. Then there's Omarosa Manigault-Stallworth of "The Apprentice," who rode the angry-black-woman stereotype to the covers of *People* and *TV Guide* magazines even as she made fellow African-American businesswomen wince.[67]

Omarosa Manigault-Stallworth gained a great deal of national disdain and celebrity as a contestant on *The Apprentice*, Donald Trump's reality show. Manigault-Stallworth, who is almost always referred to by the single name Omarosa, was portrayed (and intentionally acted) as a cross between a Jezebel—a hypersexual flirt and seductress—and a bitter, aggressive Sapphire. Lorien Olive, a political blogger, theorized on how white people saw Omarosa:

> At least among white people, she was interpreted in various ways as conniving, lazy, selfish, a sham, overly-ambitious, uppity, ungrateful, and paranoid. I guess I was always less interested in whether Omarosa was actually any of those things or whether it was simply an effect of the distortion of the editing of reality television. I was more interested in the fact that Omarosa seemed to stand for something bigger in the eyes of many white people. Her constant accusations of racism directed toward her fellow contestants and the fact that she wore her alienation and distrust of her team-mates on her sleeve opened up a whole world of racial speculation and ridicule. I would say debate, but in all of my internet travels, I haven't found much of anyone who wanted to go out on a limb for Omarosa. The fact that so many white people felt justified in their hatred for Omarosa (a hatred that could be passed of as a benign over-investment in a guilty pleasure: a reality TV series) is telling. She became the symbol of everything that went wrong in the post–Civil Rights Era: paranoid "reverse racism"; the ungrateful and undeserving product of affirmative action; the "uppity" Black person who puts on airs; the beautiful, hypersexualized Black woman who pulled the wool over the powerful white man's eyes.[68]

Olive next makes a connection that many others are making on internet sites, namely, that First Lady Michelle Obama is the new Omarosa: a bitter, selfish, uppity, ungrateful, overly ambitious Sapphire. One of the derisive nicknames for her is "Omarosa Obama." This demonstrates how the Sapphire caricature has broadened from an emasculating hater of black men to a bitter woman who hates anyone who displeases her.

CHAPTER SIX

Dangerous Men

Many caricatures of African American men portray them as menaces—dangerous, violence-prone criminals who prey on white people and undermine the larger social order. Black women are often caricatured as people who are to be pitied or exploited, while black men—as the following discussion demonstrates—are often caricatured as people to be feared and avoided.

Coon

The coon caricature is one of the most insulting of all antiblack caricatures. The name itself, an abbreviation of raccoon, is dehumanizing. As with Sambo, the coon was portrayed as a lazy, easily frightened, chronically idle, inarticulate buffoon. The coon differed from the Sambo in subtle but important ways. Sambo was depicted as a perpetual child, not capable of living as an independent adult. The coon acted childish, but he was an adult, albeit a good-for-little adult. Sambo was portrayed as a loyal and contented servant. Indeed, Sambo was offered as a defense for slavery and segregation. How bad could these institutions have been, asked the racialists, if blacks were contented, even happy, being servants? The coon, although he often worked as a servant, was not happy with his status. He was, simply, too lazy or too cynical to attempt to change his lowly position. By the 1900s, Sambo was identified with older, docile, semiliterate blacks who accepted Jim Crow laws and etiquette, whereas the coon was increasingly identified with young, urban blacks who disrespected whites. Stated differently, the coon was a Sambo gone bad.

The prototypical movie coon was Stepin Fetchit, the slow-talking, slow-walking, self-demeaning nitwit. It took his character almost a minute to say: "I'se be catchin' ma feets nah, Boss." Donald Bogle lambasted the coon, as played by Fetchit and others: "Before its death, the coon developed into the most blatantly degrading of all black stereotypes. The pure coons emerged as no-account niggers, those unreliable, crazy, lazy, subhuman creatures good for nothing more than eating watermelons, stealing chickens, shooting craps, or butchering the English language."[1]

The coon caricature was born during American slavery. Slave masters and overseers often described slaves as "slow," "lazy," "wants pushing," "an eye servant," and "trifling."[2] The master and the slave operated with different motives: the master desired to obtain from the slave the greatest labor, by any means; the enslaved person desired to do the least labor while avoiding punishment. The slave registered his protest against slavery by running away and, when that was not possible, by slowing work, doing shoddy work, destroying work tools, and faking illness. Slave masters attributed the poor work performance to shiftlessness, stupidity, desire for freedom, and genetic deficiencies.

The amount of work done by a typical slave depended upon the demands of individual slave owners and their ability to extract labor. Typically, slaves worked from dawn to dusk. They were sometimes granted "leisure time" on Saturday or Sunday evenings, but this time was spent planting or harvesting their own gardens, washing clothes, cooking, and cleaning. A slave owner wrote: "I always give them half of each Saturday, and often the whole day, at which time . . . the women do their household work; therefore they are never idle."[3]

Slave owners complained about the laziness of their workers, but the records show that slaves were often worked hard—and brutally. Overseers were routinely paid commissions, which encouraged them to overwork the slaves. On a North Carolina plantation, an overseer claimed that he was a "'hole hog man rain or shine" and boasted that the slaves had been worked "like horses." He added, "I'd ruther be dead than be a nigger on one of these big plantations."[4] After the closing of the African slave trade, the price of slaves went up, thereby causing some slave owners and their hired overseers to be more careful in their use of slaves. "The time had been," wrote one slave owner, "that the farmer could kill up and wear out one Negro to buy another; but it is not so now. Negroes are too high in proportion to the price of cotton, and it behooves those who own them to make them last as long as possible."[5]

Though slaves are generally associated with the harvest of cotton, they worked in many industries. Almost every railroad in the antebellum South was built in part by slave labor. Slaves worked in sawmills, fisheries,

A 1901 song that helped establish the derogatory term "coon" in the American vocabulary.

gold mines, and salt mines. They were used as deckhands on riverboats. They worked as lumberjacks, construction workers, longshoremen, iron workers, even store clerks. Slaves monopolized the domestic services. Some slaves worked as skilled artisans, for example, shoemakers, black-smiths, carpenters, mechanics, and barbers. These artisans were gener-ally treated better than the slaves in the cotton and tobacco fields; there-fore, it was not surprising that the artisans did better work. They included "many ingenious Mechanicks," claimed a white colonial Georgian, "and as far as they have had opportunity of being instructed, have discovered as good abilities, as are usually found among [white] people of our Colony."[6]

The supporters of slavery claimed that blacks were a childlike people unequipped for freedom. Proslavers acknowledged that some slave masters were cruel, but they argued that most were benevolent, kind-hearted capitalists who civilized and improved their inferior black wards. From Radical Reconstruction to World War I, there was a national nostalgia for the "good ol' darkies" who loved their masters and, accord-ing to the proslavers, rejected or only reluctantly accepted emancipation. In this context, the conceptualization of the coon was revised. During slavery, almost all blacks, especially men, were sometimes seen as coons, that is, lazy, shiftless, and virtually useless. However, after slavery, the

LEFT: Page from unknown book.
ABOVE: Odious image of blacks on postcard, postmarked 1907.

Goliath was struck out by David
A base hit made on Abel by Cain,

coon caricature was increasingly applied to younger blacks, especially those who were urban, flamboyant, and contemptuous of whites. Thomas Nelson Page, a white writer, wrote this in 1904:

> Universally, they [white Southerners] will tell you that while the old-time Negroes were industrious, saving, and when not misled, well-behaved, kindly, respectful, and self-respecting, and while the remnant of them who remain still retain generally these characteristics, the "new issue," for the most part, are lazy, thriftless, intemperate, insolent, dishonest, and without the most rudimentary elements of morality. . . . Universally, they report a general depravity and retrogression of the Negroes at large in sections in which they are left to themselves, closely resembling a reversion to barbarism.[7]

At the beginning of the 1900s, many whites supported the implementation of Jim Crow laws and etiquette. They believed that blacks were genetically, therefore permanently, inferior to whites. Blacks were, they argued, hedonistic children, irresponsible, and, left to their own plans, destined for idleness or savage criminality. It was not uncommon for whites to distinguish between Niggers—coons and brutes—and Negroes—mammies, Toms, and picaninnies. They preferred Negroes, actually negroes.

Racial caricatures are undergirded by stereotypes, and the stereotyping of blacks as coons continued throughout the twentieth century. A pioneering study of racial and ethnic stereotyping in the United States

DEAD GAME SPORTS.

COPYRIGHTED, 1899, AND
PUBLISHED BY KNAFFL & BRO.,
KNOXVILLE, TENN.

TOP: Be-Bop toy, 1950s.
BOTTOM: Postcard,
postmarked 1909.

POKER SERIES 36

"A TRAY FULL"

COPYRIGHT 1905 BY MAURICE WELLS

was conducted in 1933 by Daniel Katz and Kenneth Braley, two social scientists.[8] They questioned one hundred Princeton University undergraduates regarding the prevailing stereotypes of racial and ethnic groups. Their research concluded that blacks were consistently described as "superstitious," "happy-go-lucky," and "lazy." The respondents had these views even though they had little or no contact with blacks. This study was repeated in 1951, and the negative stereotyping of blacks persisted.[9] The civil rights movement improved whites' attitudes toward blacks, but a sizeable minority of whites still held traditional, racist views of blacks. An early 1990s study conducted by the National Opinion Research Center found that the majority of the white, Hispanic, and other nonblack respondents displayed negative attitudes toward blacks. For example, 78 percent said that blacks were more likely than whites to "prefer to live off welfare" and "less likely to prefer to be self-supporting." Further, 62 percent said blacks were more likely to be lazy; 56 percent said blacks were violence-prone; and 53 percent said that blacks were less intelligent than whites.[10] Stated differently, the coon caricature was still being applied to black men. Martin Gilens, a Yale University political scientist, argued that many white Americans believe that blacks receive welfare benefits more often than do whites and that "the centuries old stereotype

LEFT **TOP:** 1980s reproduction of 1940s postcard.
BOTTOM: Postcard, postmarked 1911.
ABOVE: A 1905 postcard with the portrayal of black men as happy servants.

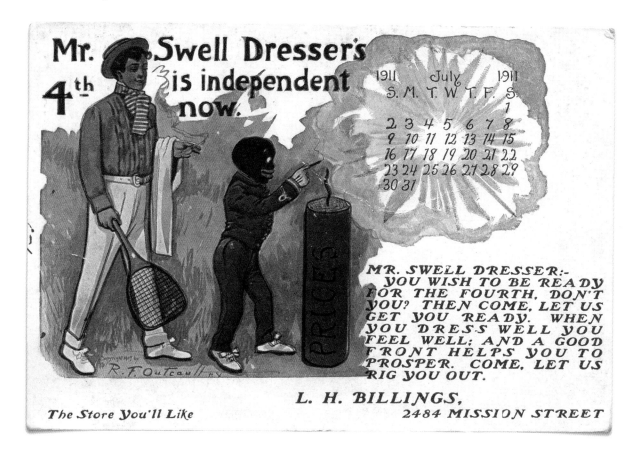

of blacks as lazy remains credible for a large number of white Americans." He claimed that opposition to welfare programs results from misinformation and racism, with whites assuming that their tax money is being used to support lazy blacks. Gilens blames, in part, the media. "Pictures of poor blacks are abundant when poverty coverage is most negative, while pictures of nonblacks dominate the more sympathetic coverage."[11]

The coon caricature was one of the stock characters among minstrel performers. Minstrel show audiences laughed at the slow-talking fool who avoided work and all adult responsibilities. This transformed the coon into a comic figure, a source of bitter and vulgar comic relief. He was sometimes renamed "Zip Coon" or "Urban Coon." If the minstrel skit had an antebellum setting, the coon was portrayed as a free black; if the skit's setting postdated slavery, he was portrayed as an urban black. He remained lazy and good-for-little, but the minstrel shows depicted him as a gaudy dressed "Dandy" who "put on airs." Unlike mammy and Sambo, the coon did not know his place. He thought he was as smart as white people, but his frequent malapropisms and distorted logic suggested that his attempt to compete intellectually with whites was pathetic. His use of bastardized English delighted white audiences and reaffirmed the then

ABOVE: A postcard, postmarked 1911.
RIGHT: Trade card with no date, Granger & Company, Buffalo, New York.

THINGS ARE NOT ALWAYS WHAT THEY SEEM.

commonly held belief that blacks were inherently stupid. The minstrel coon's goal was leisure, and his leisure was spent strutting, styling, fighting, avoiding real work, eating watermelons, and making a fool of himself. If he was married, his wife dominated him. If he was single, he sought to please the flesh without entanglements.

Hollywood films extended the brutalization inherent in the coon image. The first cinematic coon appeared in *The Wooing and Wedding of a Coon*, a racist portrayal of two mindless and stuttering buffoons. Several notable slapstick "coon shorts" were produced in 1910–1911, including *How Rastus Got His Turkey* (he stole it) and *Chicken Thief*. In the blackface comedy *Coontown Suffragettes*, a group of domineering mammies organize a "movement" to keep their good-for-nothing husbands at home. These early coons laid the foundation for the "great" movie coons of the 1930s and 1940s.[12]

In the 1929 Fox film *Hearts in Dixie*,[13] Chloe is married to Gummy, a "languid, shiftless husband whose 'mysery' in his feet prevents him from being of any earthly good as far as work is concerned, although once away from his wife's eye he can shuffle with the tirelessness and lanky abandon of a jumping jack."[14] Chloe dies of swamp fever, and Gummy remarries. The new wife is portrayed as a shrew because she tries to force Gummy

Animalistic portrayal
of African American on
140 postcard, postmarked 1908.

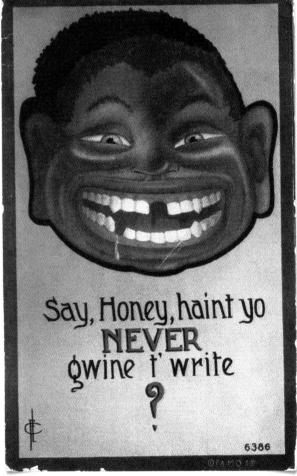

Ah've always said, and now repeat
'Ma health am due to Cream o' Whea

to work. This movie was a comedy, and most of the humor centered on Gummy's attempts to avoid work and his coon dialogue, for example, "I ain't askin you is you ain't. I is askin you is you is." The actor who played Gummy was Stepin Fetchit, the "greatest" coon actor of all time.

Stepin Fetchit was born Lincoln Theodore Perry on May 30, 1892. A medicine show and vaudeville performer, he arrived in Hollywood in the 1920s. Perry claimed that he got the name Fetchit from a racehorse that won him money. However, he also told an interviewer that he came to Hollywood as a member of a comedy team known as "Step and Fetch It" and later adopted a variant of the name. His first featured movie role using the name Stepin Fetchit was in MGM's *In Old Kentucky*.[15] Whether as Gummy, Stepin Fetchit, or other names, he essentially performed the same role: the arch-coon. Historian Daniel J. Leab wrote: "Fetchit became identified in the popular imagination as a dialect-speaking, slump-shouldered, slack-jawed character who walked, talked, and apparently thought in slow motion. The Fetchit character overcame this lethargy only when he thought that a ghost or some nameless terror might be present; and then he moved very quickly indeed."[16]

Fetchit was the embodiment of the nitwit black man. As with the Zip Coon and Urban Coon, this old-fashioned coon character could never correctly pronounce a multisyllabic word. He was portrayed as a dunce. In *Stand Up and Cheer*, he was tricked into thinking that a "talking" penguin was really Jimmy Durante.[17] Fetchit, scratching his head, eyes bulging, portrayed the coon so realistically that whites thought they were seeing a real racial type. His coon portrayal was aided by his appearance. According to Donald Bogle:

> His appearance, too, added to the caricature. He was tall and skinny and always had his head shaved completely bald. He invariably wore clothes that were too large for him and that looked as if they had been passed down from his white master. His grin was always very wide, his teeth very white, his eyes very widened, his feet very large, his walk very slow, his dialect very broken.[18]

In black communities, Stepin Fetchit remains a synonym for a bowing and scraping black man. In 1970, he sued CBS unsuccessfully for $3 million, charging defamation of character for the way he was portrayed in the television documentary *Black History: Lost, Stolen, or Strayed*.[19] "It was Step," he claimed, "who elevated the Negro to the dignity of a Hollywood star. I made the Negro a first-class citizen all over the world . . . somebody it was all right to associate with. I opened all the theaters."[20] Though that statement is hyperbole, Fetchit was a talented actor who added depth—albeit slight—to the portrayal of coons in the movies.

This Cream of Wheat advertisement was issued in 1916.

What is his legacy? He was the first black actor to receive top billing in movies and one of the first millionaire black actors. He spawned imitators, most notably Willie Best (a.k.a. Sleep 'n' Eat) and Mantan Moreland, the scared, wide-eyed manservant of Charlie Chan. In 1978, Fetchit was elected to the Black Filmmakers Hall of Fame. But he will always be remembered as the lazy, barely literate, self-demeaning, white man's black man. He attempted a comeback in the 1950s, but it was unsuccessful; his coon caricature then seemed merely embarrassing. In the late 1960s, he converted to the Black Muslim faith.

Fetchit portrayed safe coons. His movie portrayals emphasized the coon as lazy and dumb—but they de-emphasized the coon's supposed penchant for violence. The coons played by Fetchit found a willing and receptive white audience. This was the black man as a punching bag—an inarticulate, lazy buffoon who would not fight back. Fetchit's coon characters were racially demeaned and often verbally and even physically abused by white characters. In *David Harum,* he was traded to Will Rogers along with a horse. He was traded twice more in the movie. In *Judge Priest*, he was pushed, shoved, and verbally berated by Rogers. Even worse, his character was barely intelligible, scratched his head in an apelike manner, and followed Rogers around like an adoring pet.[21] But Fetchit's coon—though the most popular—was not the only coon portrayal; there was another portrayal of the coon, a depiction of black men as "niggers with razors."

Coon songs were popular in the United States and Europe from the 1880s to the 1930s. These songs, often sung by whites (and later blacks) wearing blackface makeup, portrayed blacks "as not only ignorant and indolent, but also devoid of honesty or personal honor, given to drunkenness and gambling, utterly without ambition, sensuous, libidinous, even lascivious."[22] These were songs of ridicule, songs that were the musical accompaniment to Jim Crow laws and customs. As scholar Robert Toll has explained, "Besides continuing minstrel stereotypes of blacks as watermelon- and chicken-eating mindless fools, these new 'coon songs' emphasized grotesque physical caricatures of big-lipped, pop-eyed black people and added the menacing image of razor-toting, violent black men. These lyrics almost made the romanticized plantation stereotypes seem good."[23] One of the most popular coon songs, "Leave Your Razors at the Door" (1900), offered a then-commonplace depiction of black men:

> Oh a big burly nigger by de name of Brown
> Gave a rag-time reception in des yere town
> All his friends and relations with their blades came down . . .
> When they reached the hall an awful sight they saw

A postcard, postmarked 1908, expressed the narrative that dogs hate black people.

'Twas a sign a hangin' on de big front door . . .
Ev'ry coon thought he'd drop dead
For this is what he plainly read
Leave your razors at the door
Don't yer start no rag-time war . . .
If you want some black man's gore
Don't carve him to the core
But take a good size brick and do the job up quick
Leave your razors at the door
Ev'ry coon in the party anted up his steel
Took his gal up the stairs to have a rag-time reel . . .
[A] fight was started right away
Then down the stairs a lot of coons did swoop . . .
Found that Brown and razors too had flown the coop . . .
There'll be crepe on Brown's front door
He'll never flash this sign no more.

"Leave Your Razors at the Door" and similar songs depicted blacks, especially young urban blacks, as menaces to the social order. Unlike the mammy and the Tom, there was no attempt to romanticize the coon. He was to be feared. He was a danger to others. He was a danger to whites.

Brute

Whereas the coon caricature portrays dumb, lazy black men *capable* of violence, the brute caricature portrays black men as innately savage, animalistic, destructive, and criminal—violence is a possibility for coons, it is a necessity for brutes. This brute is a fiend, a sociopath, an antisocial menace. Most of the coon's violence was directly against other blacks—as in a fight—but black brutes were portrayed as predators who targeted helpless victims, especially white women. In the 1890s the southern writer Charles H. Smith claimed, "A bad negro is the most horrible creature upon the earth, the most brutal and merciless."[24] Clifton R. Breckinridge, a former congressman and a contemporary of Smith's, said of the black race, "when it produces a brute, he is the worst and most insatiate brute that exists in human form."[25] George T. Winston, another "Negrophobic" writer, claimed, "When a knock is heard at the door [a white woman] shudders with nameless horror. The black brute is lurking in the dark, a monstrous beast, crazed with lust. His ferocity is almost demoniacal. A mad bull or tiger could scarcely be more brutal. A whole community is frenzied with horror, with the blind and furious rage for vengeance."[26]

During slavery, the dominant caricatures of blacks—mammy, coon, Tom, and picaninny—portrayed them as childlike, ignorant, docile,

groveling, and generally harmless. These portrayals were pragmatic and instrumental. Proponents of slavery created and promoted images of blacks that justified slavery and soothed white consciences. If slaves were childlike, for example, then a paternalistic institution where masters acted as quasi-parents to their slaves was humane, even morally right. More importantly, slaves were rarely depicted as brutes because that portrayal might have become a self-fulfilling prophecy.

During the Radical Reconstruction period (1867–1877), many white writers argued that without slavery—which supposedly suppressed their animalistic tendencies—blacks were reverting to criminal savagery. The belief that the newly emancipated blacks were a black peril continued into the early 1900s. Thomas Nelson Page became one of the first writers to introduce a literary black brute. In 1898, he published *Red Rock*, a Reconstruction novel, with the odious figure of Moses, a sinister black politician. Moses tried to rape a white woman: "He gave a snarl of rage and sprang at her like a wild beast."[27] He was later lynched for "a terrible crime."

The terrible crime most often mentioned in connection with the black brute was rape, specifically the rape of a white woman. At the beginning of the twentieth century, much of the virulent, antiblack propaganda that found its way into scientific journals, local newspapers, and bestselling novels focused on the stereotype of the black rapist. The claim that

This postcard, postmarked 1904, suggests that even black children are prone to violence.

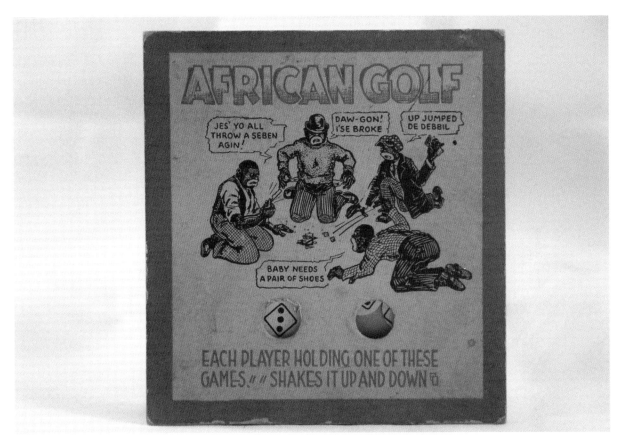

black brutes were, in epidemic numbers, raping white women became the public rationalization for the lynching of blacks.

Many of these victims were ritualistically tortured. In 1904, Luther Holbert and his wife were burned to death. They were "tied to trees and while the funeral pyres were being prepared, they were forced to hold out their hands while one finger at a time was chopped off. The fingers were distributed as souvenirs. The ears . . . were cut off. Holbert was beaten severely, his skull fractured and one of his eyes, knocked out with a stick, hung by a shred from the socket." Members of the mob then speared the victims with a large corkscrew, "the spirals tearing out big pieces of . . . flesh every time it was withdrawn."[28]

A mob lynching was a brutal and savage event, and it necessitated that the lynching victim be seen as equally brutal and savage; as these lynchings became more common and more brutal, so did the assassination of the black character. Dr. William Howard, writing in the respectable journal *Medicine* in 1903, claimed that "the attacks on defenseless white women are evidence of racial instincts" (in blacks), and the black birthright was "sexual madness and excess."[29] Thomas Dixon's *The Leopard's Spots*, a 1902 novel, claimed that emancipation had transformed

LEFT: A postcard, postmarked 1914.
TOP: 1920s dice game used for advertising.
BOTTOM: 1940s notepad.

149

blacks from "a chattel to be bought and sold into a beast to be feared and guarded."[30]

In 1905, Dixon published his most popular novel, *The Clansman*. In this book, he described the black man as "half child, half animal, the sport of impulse, whim, and conceit . . . a being who, left to his will, roams at night and sleeps in the day, whose speech knows no word of love, whose passions, once aroused, are as the fury of the tiger."[31] *The Clansman* includes a detailed and gory account of the rape of a young white virgin by a black brute. "A single tiger springs, and the black claws of the beast sank into the soft white throat." After the rape, the girl and her mother both commit suicide, and the black brute is lynched by the Ku Klux Klan. This book served as the basis for the movie *The Birth of a Nation*, which also portrayed some blacks as rapist-beasts, justified the lynching of blacks, and glorified the Ku Klux Klan.[32] Carroll, Howard, and Dixon did not exceed the prevailing racism of the so-called Progressive Era.

In 1921–22, the United States House of Representatives and Senate debated the Dyer Bill, an antilynching bill. This bill provided fines and imprisonment for persons convicted of lynching in federal courts and fines and penalties against states, counties, and cities which failed to use reasonable effort to protect citizens from lynch mobs. The Dyer Bill passed in the House of Representatives, but it was killed in the Senate by filibustering southerners who claimed that it was unconstitutional and an infringement upon states' rights.[33] The following statements made by southern congressmen during the Dyer Bill debate suggest that they were more concerned with white supremacy and the oppression of blacks than they were with constitutional issues.

Senator James Buchanan of Texas claimed that in "the Southern States and in secret meetings of the Negro race [white liberals] preach the damnable doctrine of social equality which excites the criminal sensualities of the criminal element of the Negro race and directly incites the diabolical crime of rape upon the white women. Lynching follows as swift as lightning, and all the statutes of State and Nation cannot stop it."[34]

Representative Percy Quin of Mississippi said of lynch law, "Whenever an infamous outrage is committed upon a [Southern] White woman the law is enforced, is it not, even if it happens to be enforced by the neighbors of the woman who has been outraged? The colored people of [the South] realize the manner of that enforcement, and that is the one method by which the horrible crime of rape has been held down where the Negro element is in a large majority. The man who believes that the Negro race is all bad is mistaken. But you must recollect that there is an element of barbarism in the black man, and the people around where he lives recognize that fact."[35]

Representative Thomas Sisson of Mississippi said, "As long as rape continues lynching will continue. For this crime, and this crime alone, the South has not hesitated to administer swift and certain punishment. . . . We are going to protect our girls and womenfolk from these black brutes. When these black fiends keep their hands off the throats of the women of the South then lynching will stop."[36]

Representative Benjamin Tillman from South Carolina claimed that the Dyer Bill would eliminate the states and "substitute for the starry banner of the Republic, a black flag of tyrannical centralized government . . . black as the face and heart of the rapist . . . who [recently] deflowered and killed Margaret Lear," a white girl in South Carolina.[37] Tillman asked why anyone should care about the "burning of an occasional ravisher," when the House had more important concerns.[38]

Senator T.H. Caraway of Arkansas claimed that the NAACP "wrote this bill and handed it to the proponents of it. These people had but one idea in view, and that was to make rape permissible, and to allow the guilty to go unpunished if that rape should be committed by a Negro against a white woman in the South."[39]

Despite the hyperbolic claims of those congressmen, most of the blacks lynched had not been accused of rape or attempted rape. According

Postcard, postmarked 1927. **151**

to the Tuskegee Institute's lynching data, the accusations against lynching victims for the years 1882 to 1951 were: 41 percent for felonious assault, 19.2 percent for rape, 6.1 percent for attempted rape, 4.9 percent for robbery and theft, 1.8 percent for insulting white people, and 27 percent for miscellaneous offenses (for example, trying to vote, testifying against a white man, asking a white woman to marry) or no offenses at all.[40] The 25.3 percent who were accused of rape or attempted rape were often not guilty and were killed without benefit of trial.

Lynchings often involved castration, amputation of hands and feet, spearing with long nails and sharpened steel rods, removal of eyes, beating with blunt instruments, shooting, burning at the stake, and hanging. It was, when done by southern mobs, especially sadistic, irrespective of the criminal charge. Most white southerners agreed that lynching was evil, but they claimed that black brutes were a greater evil.

Lynchings were necessary, argued many whites, to preserve the racial purity of the white race, more specifically, the racial purity of white women. White men had sexual relations, consensual and rape, with black women as soon as Africans were introduced into the European American colonies. These sexual unions produced numerous mixed-race offspring. White women, as "keepers of white racial purity," were not allowed consensual sexual relations with black men. A black man risked his life by having sexual relations with a white woman. Even talking to a white woman in a "familiar" manner could result in black males being killed.

In 1955, Emmett Till, a black fourteen-year-old from Chicago, visited his relatives in Mississippi. The exact details are not known, but Till apparently referred to a female white store clerk as "Baby." Several days later, the woman's husband and brother took Till from his uncle's home, beat him to death—his head was crushed and one eye was gouged out— and threw his body into the Tallahatchie River. The men were caught, tried, and found innocent by an all-white jury. The case became a *cause célèbre* during the civil rights movement, showing the nation that brutal violence undergirded Jim Crow laws and etiquette.

There were black rapists with white victims, but they were relatively rare; most white rape victims were raped by white men. The brute caricature was a red herring, a myth used to justify lynching, which in turn was used as a social control mechanism to instill fear in black communities. Each lynching sent messages to blacks: Do not register to vote. Do not apply for a white man's job. Do not complain publicly. Do not organize. Do not talk to white women. The brute caricature gained in popularity whenever blacks pushed for social equality. According to sociologist Allen D. Grimshaw, the most savage oppression of blacks by whites, whether expressed in rural lynchings or urban race riots, has taken place when

LEFT: "Running Nigger Target" with bullet holes, 1960s.
ABOVE: 1940s wooden head used as target in carnival games.

153

blacks have refused or been perceived by whites as refusing to accept a subordinate or oppressed status.[41]

The civil rights movement of the 1950s and 1960s forced many white Americans to examine their images of and beliefs about blacks. Television and newspaper coverage showing black protesters, including children, being beaten, arrested, and jailed by baton-waving police officers led many whites to see blacks as victims, not victimizers. The brute caricature did not die, but it lost much of its credibility. Not surprisingly, lynchings, especially public well-attended ones, decreased in number. Lynchings became "hate crimes," committed secretly. Beginning in the 1960s the relatively few blacks who were lynched were not accused of sexual assaults; instead, these lynchings were reactions of white supremacists to black economic and social progress.

The brute caricature has not been as common as the coon caricature in American movies. *The Birth of a Nation* was the first major American movie to portray all the major antiblack caricatures, including the brute.[42] That movie led to numerous black protests and white-initiated race riots. One result of the racial strife was that black male actors in the 1920s through 1940s found themselves limited to coon and Tom roles. It was neither socially acceptable nor economically profitable to show movies where black brutes terrorized whites.

In the 1960s and 1970s blaxploitation movies brought aggressive, antiwhite black males onto the big screen. Some of these fit the "buck" caricature—for example, the private detective in *Shaft* and the pimp in *Superfly*—but some of the blaxploitation actors were cinematic brutes. *American Gigolo* had a poisonous and despicable black pimp. He was one of the many black sadistic pimps who have abused and degraded whites in American movies. Mister, the husband in *The Color Purple,* is an angry and savage wife abuser, and so is Ike Turner in *What's Love Got to Do with It.* Both are brutes whose victims happen to be black. Turner's real-life criminal behavior (which predated the movie) was used to give credibility to his character's portrayal as a brute and, more importantly, to reinforce the belief that blacks are especially prone to brutish behavior.[43]

In the 1980s and 1990s, the typical cinema and television brute was nameless and sometimes faceless; he sprang from a hiding place, he robbed, raped, and murdered. He represented the cold brutality of urban life. Often he was a gangbanger. Sometimes he was a dope fiend. Actors who played the black brute were usually not on screen very long, just long enough to terrorize innocent victims. They were movie props. On television shows like *Law and Order*, *Homicide: Life on the Streets*, *ER*, and *NYPD Blue*, nameless black brutes assault, maim, and kill. On October 2, 2000, NBC debuted *Deadline,* a drama involving an irascible

Matchbook from the 1930s showing black man with oversized genitalia.

154

journalism teacher. In the first episode, two young black males brutally kill five restaurant workers. They kill without remorse. In 2001, Denzel Washington won the Best Actor Oscar for his role as a corrupt police officer in *Training Day*. Washington's character, Alonzo Harris, is one of the most despicable characters in modern cinema.[44]

During the 1988 presidential campaign, George H.W. Bush's election committee sought to portray his opponent, Michael Dukakis, as weak on crime. Bush's team used television advertisements which showed a menacing mug shot of Willie Horton, a black convicted murderer. Horton, while out of prison on an unguarded forty-eight-hour furlough, kidnapped a young white suburban couple. He repeatedly stabbed the man and raped the woman several times. The image of Horton's threatening face on the nation's television screens helped Bush win the election. It also reinforced the belief that a black brute is worse than a white brute.

> My wife's been shot. I'm shot. . . . He made us go to an abandoned area. I don't see any signs. Oh, God!

This frantic telephone call came into the Massachusetts State Police on the night of October 23, 1989. After a desperate search, using only the sound from the open cell telephone as their guide, police discovered an injured couple. Carol DiMaiti Stuart, seven months pregnant, had been shot in the head; Charles, her husband, had a serious gunshot wound to the abdomen. Hours later, doctors performed a cesarean section on the dying woman and delivered a premature baby boy who died days later. Charles Stuart told the police that the murderer was a black man.

The city of Boston, which has a history of racial discord, experienced heightened racial tensions as police searched for the black brute. Officers went into black neighborhoods and rounded up hundreds of black men for questioning. The black community was outraged. Charles Stuart picked Willie Bennett out of a lineup, and Bennett was subsequently arrested for the crime.[45] Later, police were informed by Stuart's brother that Charles Stuart probably killed his wife for insurance money. The police began investigating Charles Stuart and were building a strong circumstantial case when, on January 4, 1990, he committed suicide.

In 1994, Susan Smith, a young mother in Union, South Carolina, claimed that a man had commandeered her car with her two boys: fourteen-month-old Alex and three-year-old Michael. She described the carjacker as a "black male in his late 20s to early 30s, wearing a plaid shirt, jeans, and a toboggan-type hat." A composite of her description was published in newspapers, nationally and locally. Smith appeared on national television, tearfully begging for her sons to be returned safely. An entire nation wept with her, and the image of the black brute resurfaced. The

Reverend Mark Long, the pastor of the church where Smith's family attended services, said in reference to the black suspect, "There are some people that would like to see this man's brains bashed in."[46]

After nine days of a gut-wrenching search and strained relations between local blacks and whites, there was finally a break in the case: Susan Smith confessed to drowning her own sons. In a two-page hand-written confession, she apologized to her sons, but she did not apologize to blacks, nationally or locally. "It was hard to be black this week in Union," said Hester Booker, a local black man. "The whites acted so different. They wouldn't speak [to blacks]; they'd look at you and then reach over and lock their doors. And all because that lady lied."[47]

The false allegations of Charles Stuart and Susan Smith could have led to racial violence. In 1908, in Springfield, Illinois, Mabel Hallam, a white woman, falsely accused "a black fiend," George Richardson, of raping her. Her accusations angered local whites. They formed a mob, killed two prominent black business owners, then burned and pillaged the local black community. Blacks fled to avoid a mass lynching. Hallam later admitted that she lied about the rape to cover up an extramarital affair. How many lynchings and race riots have resulted from false accusations of rape and murder leveled against so-called black brutes?

CHAPTER SEVEN

A Night in Howell

From behind me someone yelled, "No Nazis, no KKK!" I turned to see several young men trying to force their way into the crowded room. Again, one of them shouted, "No Nazis, no KKK!" Someone in the audience, someone near the front, shouted, "Go back to Israel!" The protesters, still yelling anti-Klan slogans, were forcibly escorted from the door's entryway. The removal of the demonstrators excited the crowd. The audience had been seated in the small room for hours. A handful were on their feet venting, releasing, shouting insults. "Get out of here, Jew boy!" "This is a white man's country!" A boy two rows up—he looked like he was fourteen or fifteen years old—stood on his chair and gave the Hitler salute. An older man sitting near me—one of the people who had arranged for me to come to the auction—looked at me as if to say, "Don't worry, everything will be fine." I sat there thinking: *What the hell am I doing in Howell, Michigan? The Jim Crow Museum already has three Klan robes.*

If I had my druthers, there would be only scant attention devoted to the Ku Klux Klan in the Jim Crow Museum. One major lesson of the museum is that racism is not limited to white supremacist terrorists. The Jim Crow Museum focuses on the commonplace objects—postcards, games, drinking glasses, detergent, lawn jockeys, and other everyday objects—that reflected and shaped attitudes about African Americans. The Klan did not create the millions of objects sold in stores which depicted blacks as loyal servants, pitiable buffoons, self-loathing mulattoes, or dangerous savages. These objects were, in the main, created, distributed, and purchased by Americans who disavowed the Ku Klux Klan. Though the museum does not focus on the Klan, one cannot accurately

analyze the history of race relations in this country without including KKK material, so we have always had a small amount of it.

When I moved to Michigan in 1990, Howell had the reputation of being a city hostile to African Americans and other racial minorities. That reputation was cemented, in part, by the activities of Robert E. Miles, who was a former Grand Dragon of the Ku Klux Klan. Miles owned a seventy-acre farm in Cohoctah Township, a rural township several miles north of Howell. Klansmen and other white supremacists from across the country traveled to Miles's farm; they fraternized, shared ideas, listened to Miles lecture, and burned crosses. Some of the attending Klansmen were from Howell and nearby towns. Those Klansmen who traveled great distances "would stream through Howell, check in to the Holiday Inn and trek to the farm for their meetings."[1] The gatherings occurred in the 1970s and 1980s, and although they were not within the Howell city limits, they helped brand Howell as a haven for Klansmen and other white supremacists.

The first Ku Klux Klan group emerged after the Civil War, and soon thereafter, they were using violence to intimidate newly freed black people. Floggings, rapes, and murders were tools of social control used to

Photographs from a Klan initiation, 1960s.

return African Americans to a state of bondage. There have been at least five incarnations of the Klan. Before the 1940s, the Klan was a monolithic organization, but in later years the national Klan was replaced by several autonomous Klan organizations. The organizational structure of Klan life changed but not their use of violence. In 1971, Miles and four associates were convicted of conspiracy to bomb school buses that were to be used for court-ordered desegregation in Pontiac, Michigan. Two years later, he was convicted on a conspiracy charge related to the tarring and feathering of a Willow Run High School principal. He spent six years in federal prison for the crimes. Later in his life, Miles embraced a political-theological ideology known as Christian Identity. Led by Miles and Richard Butler, Christian Identity was an attempt to use a whites-centric version of Christianity to unite Klansmen with members of other white supremacist groups, most notably neo-Nazis, the Aryan Nations, and Posse Comitatus—all domestic terrorists. Miles loathed the U.S. federal government, and he hated blacks and other minorities. His solution was the Northwest Imperative—the call for whites to migrate to the Pacific Northwest and create a white state. His hatred of the federal government and his white supremacist ideology led to some people calling him a "klanarchist."[2]

Miles died in 1992, and there are community leaders in Howell who would like to see his legacy die. This is why they invited me to come to the auction. They wanted to make a symbolic gesture to demonstrate their disapproval of the Klan and what it symbolizes. The Livingston County 2001 Diversity Council, under the leadership of Vic Lopez, had originally planned to win the robe at auction—and then burn it. Professor K. Miller, one of my colleagues at Ferris, read about their plan and told the Diversity Council that the Klan robe should not be destroyed but should be donated to the Jim Crow Museum so that we could use it to teach tolerance and promote social justice. The Diversity Council agreed.

Someone would have to bid on the robe. The Diversity Council worried that Klan sympathizers would not let one of the Council's members win the bid because of their earlier threat to destroy it. After several conversations between Professor Miller and community leaders in Howell, it was decided that Jim Crow Museum representatives would come to Howell, bid on the robe, presumably win the bid, and then have the Diversity Council reimburse the bid amount and donate the robe to the museum.

A Klan robe for auction in Howell is newsworthy. The local Howell newspaper, the *Livingston County Daily Press & Argus*, ran almost daily accounts of the escalating drama. Opinions about the robe divided the community. Media from Lansing, Detroit, and Ann Arbor covered the impending auction. The newspaper and television coverage was noticed by others who had Klan memorabilia to sell; indeed, by the night of the auction, there were approximately a dozen robes for sale, along with knives, swords, T-shirts, photographs, souvenirs, pamphlets, and other oddball objects: all emblazoned with KKK images or messages.[3] And the media coverage quickly went national, which, among other things, assured that dozens of gawkers, protesters, and bidders—some racist, some not—would be joining me in Howell.

Howell is situated between Ann Arbor, Detroit, Lansing, and Flint. It is, for many of its almost ten thousand residents, a charming, almost idyllic little city. It is a city in love with the arts, cultural programs, and festivals. Each summer, the city hosts a Harry Potter celebration. Howell is known for the Michigan Balloonfest Challenge, a hot air balloon festival held every June. There is also the Howell Melon Festival, a celebration of a cantaloupe that grows nearby. The three-day festival, held in mid-August, attracts nearly fifty thousand visitors. At the renovated Howell Opera House, one will find the Livingston Arts Council, the inspiration behind many of the city's family friendly activities. From a distance—maybe even from up close—Howell is a pleasant, wholesome community, but that was not my experience on the evening of January 29, 2005. As I sat in the Ole Gray Nash Auction House in downtown Howell—a downtown district that is listed in the National Registry of Historic Places—I did not have the Rotary Club vision of Howell. Like many cities, Howell has a split personality.

The Ole Gray Auction House seats approximately one hundred people comfortably, but more than two hundred crammed into the room to wait for the auction. Professor Miller and I got there three hours before the auction so that we were assured of having seats. While I protected our seats, Professor Miller met with members of the Diversity Council and other city leaders to finalize the details of our arrangement, especially our role as purchasing agents. The fire marshal came and threatened to close the auction if people did not leave; a couple of people left, probably because of the heat in the room. There was, in my opinion, little chance that the fire marshal or city officials would enforce the building codes; too many people had traveled too far from too many places. Seats were precious.

By the time Professor Miller returned, I was agitated. For an hour and a half, I was hassled for saving the seat for a friend. That was the least of it. Several people stood behind me, arms folded, so close I could hear their breathing. They were trying to intimidate me. Others stared at me and silently mouthed words that were laden with profanity and racial epithets. To make matters worse, the auctioneer gave an impromptu speech, which included a reference to "showing this town a real parade,"

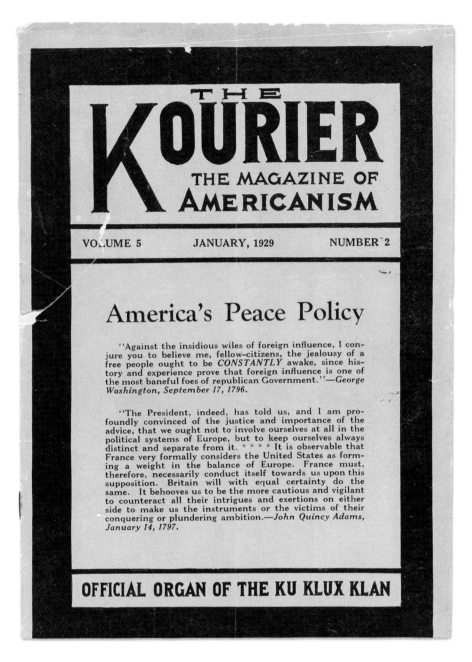

THE

KOURIER

THE MAGAZINE OF
AMERICANISM

VOLUME 5   JANUARY, 1929   NUMBER 2

America's Peace Policy

"Against the insidious wiles of foreign influence, I con-jure you to believe me, fellow-citizens, the jealousy of a free people ought to be *CONSTANTLY* awake, since his-tory and experience prove that foreign influence is one of the most baneful foes of republican Government."—*George Washington, September 17, 1796.*

"The President, indeed, has told us, and I am pro-foundly convinced of the justice and importance of the advice, that we ought not to involve ourselves at all in the political systems of Europe, but to keep ourselves always distinct and separate from it. * * * * It is observable that France very formally considers the United States as form-ing a weight in the balance of Europe. France must, therefore, necessarily conduct itself towards us upon this supposition. Britain will with equal certainty do the same. It behooves us to be the more cautious and vigilant to counteract all their intrigues and exertions on either side to make us the instruments or the victims of their conquering or plundering ambition.—*John Quincy Adams, January 14, 1797.*

OFFICIAL ORGAN OF THE KU KLUX KLAN

which was an allusion to a previous Klan march, which the town's people had largely thwarted by closing local businesses.

When the auction finally began, I was excited. I had every intention to bid on the robe at the center of the controversy, and I expected to pay maybe $300. In 1992, I was one of the bidders at an auction in Fremont, Michigan. There, I bought a Klan robe for $80. I expected the media attention to drive up the demand for the Howell robe, but I was surprised to see the bidding go over $500, and I certainly was no longer interested when it went over $1,000. I watched in amazement as a simple Klan

Johnny Rebel is the pseudonym of Clifford Joseph Trahan, who made racist recordings in the 1960s on the Reb Rebel label.

robe eventually reached the pricey sum of $1,425. Another Klan robe sold for more than $1,000.

The Diversity Council members were worried that I was not going to "win" a bid for a robe. They did not want to leave the auction empty-handed. I understood, but I wanted to get something that the Jim Crow Museum "needed"—and the only remaining item that I could rationalize needing was a Klanswoman's robe. Although it is often seen as a white adult male organization, the Klan has included women since the 1920s—the period of the Klan's greatest popularity. In that decade, the Women of the Ku Klux Klan (WKKK) was a Klan auxiliary that existed in every state.[4] Like their male counterparts, the WKKK was anti-black, anti-Jewish, anti-Catholic, and anti-immigrant. They did not use violence as often as men—but they did sometimes use violence to get what they wanted. Although there were several hundred thousand Klanswomen in the 1920s, the robes are rarely seen at auctions.

When the bidding for the woman's robe began, it was clear that it would come down to me and a white woman sitting on the front row. I knew that I would have to overspend. All the winning bidders overpaid that night. KKK knives that one could purchase on eBay for $20 sold for hundreds at the auction. A raggedy Klan T-shirt sold for $80. A blue Klan officer's robe from Kentucky was sold with a sword; together, they sold for more than $5,000.

I won the bid for the woman's robe at $700. The next day, my purchase was reported in an Associated Press story about the auction. Almost immediately, the Jim Crow Museum received letters from people across the country trying to sell Klan regalia. I suppose they assumed if I was foolish enough to purchase a robe for that price, I might be imprudent enough to purchase their robes at similar prices. I did not purchase any of the offered robes, but the publicity did result in the museum receiving several collections that included Klan robes.

When we left the auction, there were still many gawkers, protesters, and media personnel near the building. The media had not been allowed in the auction house. One reporter, a woman from a television station,

TOP: Klan certificate from
New Jersey chapter, 1986.
BOTTOM: The Reb-Time
label and songs have been
recently recorded and
placed online.

walked up to me and asked, "What are you doing here?" Her tone was
accusatory. I explained that I was the founder of the Jim Crow Museum
and that we had been invited to Howell by a local diversity committee to act as a purchasing agent and that
they planned to donate the object to the museum.
I believe it was during this interview that I
said, "I felt like I was at a Klan rally at some
times." That quote appeared in newspapers across the country.[5]

My colleague and I crossed the
street to give the robe to representatives of the Livingston 2001
Diversity Committee. We were told
that the ceremonial presentation of
the robe would occur at the Howell
Opera House within the hour. I
did not like that development. I
wanted to go home. As we walked
to the opera house, we passed four
teenagers. One of them looked at me
and said, "If it ain't white, it ain't right."
I prepared to defend myself, but they

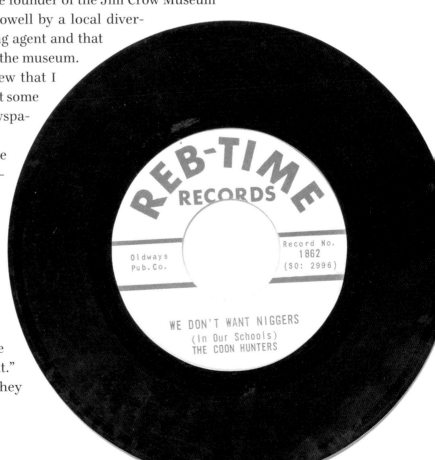

laughed and walked away. It was cold, Michigan cold, and as dark as it gets. After the incident with the teenagers, I became vigilant. I watched every person that came close to me. The short walk to the Howell Opera House seemed like a long walk.

While the auction was going on, a group of citizens held a candle-light vigil. Many of those people were now in the opera house. Two boys, very little boys, were playing together near the door's entryway. Some people were watching the video *Not in Our Town*, others were chatting in small groups, still others were praying. I sat until I was called forward to address the audience. I don't remember what I said, but I do remember what I tried to say.

Hatred is a powerful organizing force, and that is an unfortunate truth. But, those in hate groups in the United States lost the cultural battle. They will never offer a concession speech, but they lost. They are relics. Their hate is fueled by fear—fear of a world where privileges and social goodies are not handed to you solely because you are white; fear of honest competition from people who are brown, yellow, black, or red; fear of not knowing what the future holds. They hate me because I exist. I most assuredly exist, and I exist in this country. This is my home, the home of my sweat, the home of my hopes. I am not going anywhere. In the past, the Klan wrapped their gospel of white supremacy in a perverted version of Christianity—claiming that God was a segregationist. They burned crosses and claimed that the desecration honored Jesus Christ. And they used violence as an instrument, a tool to suppress blacks and other so-called undesirables. Hurting us was their ego boost, but those days are over. Today the message of the Klan is the same (the tone is occasionally softer), but their combustible discourse plays to sparse crowds. That is good. Thank you for sending a message, loud and clear, to the purveyors of terror. Thank you for standing up to hooded bigotry, but now I need you to shift focus. Most of the Klan sympathizers will leave, but it is up to you to build a community that belongs to its entire people as much as it belongs to any of its individual members. Yes, build a community that rejects Klan and Nazi membership, but more importantly, build a community where peoples of color can live and work without being mistreated, where they can rear families, get jobs—good paying jobs—send their children to good schools, have their work appreciated, live peaceful lives. The hard work is the everyday work, the work that the media does not cover. You can do this; we can help.

I was done, spent, and against my best efforts, crying. On my way to my seat, I again noticed the two young children playing. They were kneeling on the floor, arranging and rearranging blocks on a table. They were beautiful little boys, so young, so innocent. I wondered if they would grow up to hate black people.

I purchased these photographs at the 1992 auction in Fremont, Michigan.

Form III

KLORAN

or

RITUAL of

The WOMEN

of the

KU KLUX KLAN

7324

IMPERIAL HEADQUARTERS

WOMEN *of the* KU KLUX KLAN

LITTLE ROCK, ARKANSAS

PARKE-HARPER PUB. CO., LITTLE ROCK

A year later, the Jim Crow Museum brought the *Hateful Things* traveling exhibition to the Howell Opera House. We did not charge rental or transportation fees. It was our way of saying thank you for the Klan robe and, more importantly, thank you for standing against racism.

Each year, Ferris State University and the Jim Crow Museum award a Martin Luther King Jr. Social Justice Award to individuals and organizations that live out Dr. King's commitment to social justice. In 2006, the award was given to the Livingston 2001 Diversity Council. This grassroots organization—made up of clergy, educators, government officials, businesspeople, and private citizens—has the mission of making their community more welcoming, harmonious, and prosperous for people of all races, creeds, and backgrounds. The Diversity Council works to not only change the image of Howell and other cities in the county, but also to change the actual behaviors that led to the branding of the area as a hotbed of white supremacy. Not insignificantly, the Council was created in 1988 in response to a cross-burning in the yard of a black family in Livingston County.

I rarely talk about that night in Howell. But recently I shared those experiences with a group that visited the museum. There were two dozen of them, all African Americans and all elderly. They were, to a person, first- or second-generation northerners, more specifically, they or their parents had migrated to Detroit from the Deep South—fleeing boll weevils, rural poverty, and unfiltered racial hatred. They had come to Detroit to create lives that were materially better. Many had found ghettos. There was precious little that I could *teach* them about Jim Crow.

Many years earlier—when building the museum was only a vague hope—I worried that African Americans, particularly those who had lived during Jim Crow, would not support a museum that focused on racist objects. I worried that my African American elders would see the facility as an unnecessary reminder, a worthless shrine to racism. And, quite frankly, those worries briefly returned as I spoke with the group from Detroit.

For more than an hour I talked about that night in Howell. I explained why I went, why I stayed, and how the night impacted me and others. They sat, listened, occasionally a question was asked, but, in the main, they were silent as they listened. When I finished talking, one by one, they came up to me and said thank you. As I looked into their faces, I realized that they were, indeed, appreciative of the museum and its work, and that, for me, was all the validation I would ever need.

Professor Jon McDonald, an artist at Kendall College of Art and Design of Ferris State University, painted the *Cloud of Witnesses* in 2012. The witnesses featured in the clouds comprise a small but diverse collection of individuals who were killed during the civil rights movement.

Johnnie Mae Chappell (1929–1964), a thirty-five-year-old wife and mother, lived in Pickettville, a poor black neighborhood near Jacksonville, Florida. On March 23, 1964, race riots raged in downtown Jacksonville. Several young white men, angry about the racial tensions, decided to "get a nigger." They murdered Chappell, who was on a roadside looking for a wallet she had lost.

Michael Henry Schwerner (1939–1964), **James Earl Chaney** (1943–1964), and **Andrew Goodman** (1943–1964) were civil rights activists helping to register African Americans to vote in Mississippi. On June 21, 1964, they were arrested on trumped-up charges, imprisoned for several hours, and then released at night into the hands of Klansmen, who tortured and murdered them.

James Reeb (1927–1965), a white Unitarian Universalist minister, died on March 11, 1965, in Selma, Alabama, two days after being savagely beaten by white men with clubs. He had traveled to Selma to support voting rights for African Americans. President Lyndon B. Johnson invoked Reeb's memory when he delivered a draft of the Voting Rights Act to Congress. The act was passed into law on August 6, 1965.

Delano Herman Middleton (1951–1968), **Samuel Ephesians Hammond Jr.** (1950–1968), and **Henry Ezekiel Smith** (1950–1968) were African American teenagers killed by police during a civil rights protest on February 8, 1968, in Orangeburg, South Carolina. This tragedy came to be known as the Orangeburg Massacre.

Viola Gregg Liuzzo (1925–1965), a wife and mother from Detroit, was so moved by televised reports of civil rights protesters in Alabama being beaten that she drove there to join the movement. She was transporting marchers between Selma and Montgomery when she was killed by shots fired by Klansmen in a passing car. She is believed to be the only white woman martyred during the modern civil rights movement.

Medgar Evers (1925–1963) was an NAACP field director and a leader of boycotts and other protests in Mississippi. On June 12, 1963, a sniper shot Evers in his driveway. He was taken to a hospital in Jackson. The hospital workers initially refused him service because of his race. Then, realizing his national prominence, they gave him medical attention. He died in the hospital less than an hour after arriving.

Ben Chester White (1899–1966) was an African American who spent most of his life working on a farm in Natchez, Mississippi. He was apolitical and not a civil rights worker. On June 10, 1966, he was killed by Klansmen who hoped his murder would bring Martin Luther King Jr. to Natchez so that the Klan could kill the civil rights leader.

Denise McNair (1951–1963), **Addie Mae Collins** (1949–1963), **Cynthia Wesley** (1949–1963), and **Carole Robertson** (1949–1963) were killed when Ku Klux Klan members bombed the Sixteenth Street Baptist Church in Birmingham, Alabama, on September 15, 1963. Their deaths focused national attention on racial violence in the United States, especially the South.

Malcolm X (1925–1965), born Malcolm Little and also known as el-Hajj Malik el-Shabazz, was one of this country's most articulate and forceful advocates for racial justice. *The Autobiography of Malcolm X*, written with Alex Haley, is one of the most influential books of the twentieth century. Although there is some dispute surrounding the circumstances of his death, the general consensus is that he was killed by members of the Nation of Islam.

Martin Luther King Jr. (1929–1968) was arguably the most influential civil rights and human rights advocate of the twentieth century. Trained as a theologian, King is hailed for his use of nonviolent and civil disobedience approaches to undermining Jim Crow segregation. He was killed on April 4, 1968, while in Memphis, Tennessee, to support striking sanitation workers.

About the Museum

The Jim Crow Museum, located at Ferris State University, is the nation's largest publicly accessible collection of racist artifacts, primarily but not exclusively segregation-related memorabilia. These objects are used as tools to facilitate a deeper understanding of historical and contemporary patterns and expressions of racism. The museum is a resource for scholars, students, civil rights activists, and media, including the *New York Times*, Associated Press, British Broadcasting Corporation, National Public Radio, and many others. To learn more about the museum, visit www.ferris.edu/jimcrow.

About the Author

Dr. David Pilgrim is a public speaker and one of this country's leading experts on issues relating to multiculturalism, diversity, and race relations. He is best known as the founder and curator of the Jim Crow Museum. Dr. Pilgrim is a recipient of Ferris State University's Distinguished Teacher Award and has delivered public lectures at dozens of institutions, among them Stanford University, Colby College, the University of Michigan, Smith College, and the University of North Carolina. He is an applied sociologist who challenges audiences to think deeply about diversity and race relations. His goal is to get people talking about diversity and race relations in meaningful ways, and then to go and do something positive.

Notes

CHAPTER ONE

1   Stetson Kennedy, *Jim Crow Guide: The Way It Was* (Boca Raton: Florida Atlantic University Press, 1990), 234. This book, originally published in 1959, is a profound—albeit often satirical—critique of the racial hierarchy that operated during the Jim Crow period.

2   I saw a copy of the puzzle in 2012 at the Mark Twain House in Hartford, Connecticut. They were hosting the Jim Crow Museum's *Hateful Things* exhibition and added complementary objects to the exhibition.

3   Janette Faulkner et al., *Ethnic Notions: Black Images in the White Mind: An Exhibition of Afro-American Stereotype and Caricature from the Collection of Janette Faulkner: September 12–November 4, 1982* (Berkeley: Berkeley Art Center, 1982), 11. The images in this book inspired Marlon Riggs's documentary *Ethnic Notions*.

4   See C. Vann Woodward, *The Strange Career of Jim Crow* (New York: Oxford University Press, 1974). This book remains a classic critique of Jim Crow laws and etiquette. Or read Isabel Wilkerson, *The Warmth of Other Suns: The Epic Story of America's Great Migration* (New York: Random House, 2010). Wilkerson's portrayal of Jim Crow oppression is thorough and accurate.

5   Paul Robeson, *Here I Stand* (Boston: Beacon Press, 1971).

6   When I was a teenager, we used to refer to Birmingham as Bombingham because of the association of the city with terrorism against blacks.

7   Marlon Riggs, *Ethnic Notions* (California Newsreel, 1986); Clayton Rye, *Jim Crow's Museum* (Grim Rye Productions, 2004).

8   Andrew Macdonald, *The Turner Diaries* (New York: Barricade Books Inc., 1996).

9   As founder of the National Alliance, the largest neo-Nazi organization in this country, Pierce used weekly radio addresses, the internet, white power music ventures, and racist video games to promote his vision of a whites-only homeland and a government free of "non-Aryan influence." Pierce died on July 23, 2002, but his followers have vowed to carry on his work.

10   Keith Boykin, "Protests Close Shirley Q. Liquor Drag Minstrel Show," http://www.keithboykin.com/arch000488.html, accessed 4 March 2004.

CHAPTER TWO

1   This was a term made popular by the sociologist E. Franklin Frazier in his book *Black Bourgeoisie* (New York: Glencoe, IL: 1957). When it was first published, *Black Bourgeoisie* was reviled and revered—revered for its skillful analysis of an emerging black middle class, reviled for its blunt criticism of them.

CHAPTER THREE

1   For further information on minstrels, see: Annemarie Bean, James Vernon Hatch, and Brooks McNamara, *Inside the Minstrel Mask: Readings in Nineteenth-Century Blackface Minstrelsy* (Hanover, NH: Wesleyan University Press, 1996); Dale Cockrell, *Demons of Disorder: Early Blackface Minstrels and Their World* (Cambridge; New York: Cambridge University Press, 1997); Lester S. Levy, *Picture the Songs: Lithographs from the Sheet Music of Nineteenth-Century America* (Baltimore: Johns Hopkins University Press, 1976); Robert C. Toll, *Blacking Up: The Minstrel Show in Nineteenth-Century America* (New York: Oxford University Press, 1974).

2   Stetson Kennedy, *Jim Crow Guide: The Way It Was*, 2nd ed. (Boca Raton: Florida Atlantic Press, 1990).

3   This list was derived from a larger list compiled by the Martin Luther King Jr. National Historic Site Interpretive Staff. "Jim Crow Laws," accessed March 14, 2013, http://www.nps.gov/malu/forteachers/jim_crow_laws.htm.

4   Gunnar Myrdal, *An American Dilemma* (New York: Harper, 1944), 560–61.

5   Ibid., 561–62.

6   Arthur Franklin Raper and Southern Commission on the Study of Lynching, *The Tragedy of Lynching* (Chapel Hill: University of North Carolina Press, 1933), 13–14.

7   Myrdal, *An American Dilemma*, 566.

8   W.E.B. Du Bois, *Writings*, ed. Nathan Irvin Huggins (New York: The Library of America, 1986), 747.

9   Joseph Boskin, *Urban Racial Violence in the Twentieth Century* (Beverly Hills: Glencoe Press, 1976), 14–15.

10 George M. Fredrickson, *The Black Image in the White Mind: The Debate on Afro-American Character and Destiny, 1817–1914* (New York: Harper & Row, 1971), 272.

CHAPTER FOUR

1   Catherine Clinton, *The Plantation Mistress: Woman's World in the Old South* (New York: Pantheon Books, 1982), 201–2.

2   Patricia A. Turner, *Ceramic Uncles & Celluloid Mammies: Black Images and Their Influence on Culture* (New York: Anchor Books, 1994), 44.

3   Jo Ann Gibson Robinson and David J. Garrow, *The Montgomery Bus Boycott and the Women Who Started It: The Memoir of Jo Ann Gibson Robinson* (Knoxville: University of Tennessee Press, 1987), 107.

4   Barbara Christian, *Black Women Novelists: The Development of a Tradition, 1892–1976* (Westport, CT: Greenwood Press, 1980), 11–12.

5   D.W. Griffith, *The Birth of a Nation* (David W. Griffith Corp, 1915); Thomas Dixon, *The Clansman: An Historical Romance of the Ku Klux Klan* (New York: Grosset & Dunlap, 1905); Victor Fleming, *Gone with the Wind* (Selznick International Pictures, 1940).

6   Harriet Beecher Stowe, *Uncle Tom's Cabin* (New York: New American Library, 1966), 31.

7   Alan Crosland, *The Jazz Singer* (Warner Bros. Pictures, 1927).

8   John M. Stahl, *Imitation of Life* (Universal Pictures, 1934).

9   Donald Bogle, *Toms, Coons, Mulattoes, Mammies, and Bucks: An Interpretive History of Blacks in American Films* (New York: Continuum, 1994), 57.

10 Lowell Sherman, *She Done Him Wrong* (Paramount Pictures, 1933); *Bombshell* (Metro-Goldwyn-Mayer, 1933); John Cromwell, *Made for Each Other* (Selznick International Pictures, 1939); H.C. Potter, *Mr. Blandings Builds His Dream House* (RKO Radio Pictures, 1948).

11   Douglas Sirk, *Imitation of Life* (Universal International Pictures, 1959).

12   David Howard, *The Golden West* (Fox Film Corporation, 1932); Stephen Roberts, *The Story of Temple Drake* (Paramount Pictures, 1933); John Ford, *Judge Priest* (Fox Film Corporation, 1934); George Marshall, *Music Is Magic* (Fox Film Corporation, 1935); David Butler, *The Little Colonel* (Fox Film Corporation, 1935); George Stevens, *Alice Adams* (RKO Radio Pictures, 1935); Jack Conway, *Saratoga* (Metro-Goldwyn-Mayer, 1937); Leigh Jason, *The Mad Miss Manton* (RKO Radio Pictures, 1938).

13   Bogle, *Toms, Coons, Mulattoes, Mammies, and Bucks*, 82.

14   Stanley Sacharow, *Symbols of Trade: Your Favorite Trademarks and the Companies They Represent* (New York: Art Direction Book Co., 1982), 82.

15   Bogle, *Toms, Coons, Mulattoes, Mammies, and Bucks*, 5–6.

16   Stowe, *Uncle Tom's Cabin*, 439.

17   Ibid., 508.

18   Ibid., 509.

19   Turner, *Ceramic Uncles & Celluloid Mammies*, 78.

20   Ibid., 73.

21   Ibid.

22   Edwin S. Porter, *Uncle Tom's Cabin* (Edison Manufacturing Company, 1903); William Robert Daly, *Uncle Tom's Cabin* (World Film, 1914); Harry A. Pollard, *Uncle Tom's Cabin* (Universal Pictures, 1928).

23   Bogle, *Toms, Coons, Mulattoes, Mammies, and Bucks*, 6; Sidney Olcott, *Confederate Spy* (Kalem Company, 1910); Joseph A. Golden, *For Massa's Sake* (Pathé Frères, 1911); Paul Sloane, *Hearts in Dixie* (Fox Film Corporation, 1929).

24   David Butler, *The Littlest Rebel* (Twentieth Century Fox Film Corporation, 1935); Butler, *The Little Colonel*; George Marshall, *In Old Kentucky*, (Fox Film Corporation, 1935); Irving Cummings, *Just Around the Corner* (Twentieth Century Fox Film Corporation, 1938).

25   Bogle, *Toms, Coons, Mulattoes, Mammies, and Bucks*, 54; James Whale, *Show Boat* (Universal Pictures, 1936); Aubrey Scotto, *Follow Your Heart* (Republic Pictures, 1936); Harold D. Schuster, *Zanzibar* (Universal Pictures, 1940); Ernst Lubitsch, *Heaven Can Wait* (Twentieth Century Fox Film Corporation, 1943); Reginald Le Borg, *Joe Palooka in the Knockout* (Monogram Pictures, 1947); Frank Capra, *Riding High* (Paramount Pictures, 1950).

26   William Wyler, *Jezebel* (Warner Bros. Pictures, 1938); George Marshall, *You Can't Cheat an Honest Man* (Universal Pictures, 1939); Mark Sandrich, *Love Thy Neighbor* (Paramount Pictures, 1940); Sidney Lanfield, *The Meanest Man in the World* (Twentieth Century Fox Film Corporation, 1943).

27   Bogle, *Toms, Coons, Mulattoes, Mammies, and Bucks*, 176; Martin Ritt, *Edge of the City* (Metro-Goldwyn-Mayer, 1957); Stanley Kramer, *The Defiant Ones* (Curtleigh Productions, 1958); Ralph Nelson, *Lilies of the Field* (Rainbow Productions, 1963); Sydney Pollack, *The Slender Thread* (Stephen Alexander Productions, 1966); Guy Green, *A Patch of Blue* (Metro-Goldwyn-Mayer, 1965); James Clavell, *To Sir, with Love* (Columbia Pictures Corporation, 1967).

28   Nevertheless this movie broke new ground. The romantic pairing of a black man with a white woman was still controversial in the 1960s. Indeed, it was not until 1967, in *Loving v. Virginia*, that the United States Supreme Court ruled laws which forbade interracial marriages to be unconstitutional.

29   Daniel Petrie, *A Raisin in the Sun* (Columbia Pictures Corporation, 1961); Stanley Kramer, *Guess Who's Coming to Dinner* (Columbia Pictures Corporation, 1967).

30   Bruce Beresford, *Driving Miss Daisy* (The Zanuck Company, 1989); Jon Avnet, *Fried Green Tomatoes* (Act III Communications, 1991).

31   Quentin Tarantino, *Django Unchained* (The Weinstein Company, 2012).

32   The name *Rastus* is probably derived from *Eratus*; both were fairly common names for American blacks at the end of the 1800s. Rastus appears in many antiblack jokes before the 1960s.

33   M.A. Siegel, "Classic Trademarks Put Best Faces Forward," *Marketing News* 26 (July 6, 1992): 17.

34   G. Baker-Fletcher, "Xodus Musings: Reflections on Womanist Tar Baby Theology," *Theology Today* 50, no. 1 (1993): 39.

35   "Bayard Rustin: Obituary," *New Republic* 197 (September 28, 1987): 10.

36   "Uncle Thomas, Lawn Jockey for the Far Right?," *Emerge* 8, no. 2 (November 1996).

37   J. Goldberg, "Politics & Pugilists," *Commentary Magazine* (June 1997).

38   Ibid.

39   Ali used this tactic to motivate himself. Terrell, a fine fighter, was the underdog.

40   Tex Maule, "Cruel Ali with All the Skills," February 13, 1967, http://sportsillustrated. cnn.com/vault/article/magazine/MAG1079523/index.htm.

41   Jason Hehir, *The Fab Five* (ESPN, 2011).

42   Cornel West, *Race Matters* (Boston: Beacon Press, 1993); "Open Letter to Cornel West & the Other Uncle Toms from the African United Front (1993)," accessed March 15, 2013, http://www.blacksandjews.com/OpenLetterCornelWest.html; "Tavis Smiley and Cornel West Criticize President Obama, Steve Harvey Responds," accessed March 17, 2013, http://www.essence.com/2011/08/13/tavis-smiley-and-cornel-west-criticize-president-obama-steve-harvey-responds.

43   It is also spelled pickaninny and piccaninny.

44   See David Pilgrim, "Coon Caricature," 2000, http://www.ferris.edu/jimcrow/coon/.

45   Stowe, *Uncle Tom's Cabin*, 258.

46   Turner, *Ceramic Uncles & Celluloid Mammies*, 14.

47   Bogle, *Toms, Coons, Mulattoes, Mammies, and Bucks*, 7.

48   Edwin S. Porter, *Ten Pickaninnies* (Edison Manufacturing Company, 1908).

49   Robert F. McGowan, *Our Gang* (Hal Roach Studios, 1922).

50   Daniel J. Leab, *From Sambo to Superspade: The Black Experience in Motion Pictures* (Boston: Houghton Mifflin Co., 1976).

51   Bogle, *Toms, Coons, Mulattoes, Mammies, and Bucks*, 23.

52   W.F. McLaughlin & Co. and Koerner & Hayes, *The Ten Little Niggers.* (Chicago: W.F. McLaughlin & Co., 1890).

53   William Benjamin Smith, *The Color Line: A Brief in Behalf of the Unborn* (New York: McClure, Phillips & Co., 1905).

54   George M. Fredrickson, *The Black Image in the White Mind: The Debate on Afro-American Character and Destiny, 1817–1914* (New York: Harper & Row, 1971), 257.

55   Ibid., 71–164.

56   A pinback is similar to a brooch, but it has a flat face to display an advertisement or other image.

57   Turner, *Ceramic Uncles & Celluloid Mammies*, 15.

CHAPTER FIVE

1   A mulatto is defined as the first general offspring of a black and white parent or an individual with both white and black ancestors. Generally, mulattoes are light-skinned, though dark enough to be excluded from the white race.

2   William Wells Brown and Robert S. Levine, *Clotel; or, The President's Daughter: A Narrative of Slave Life in the United States* (Boston: Bedford/St. Martin's, 2000).

3   Vera Caspary, *The White Girl* (New York: J.H. Sears & Co., 1929); Geoffery Barnes, *Dark Lustre* (New York: AH King, 1932).

4   John M. Stahl, *Imitation of Life* (Universal Pictures, 1934).

5   Douglas Sirk, *Imitation of Life* (Universal International Pictures, 1959).

6   Edward Byron Reuter, *The Mulatto in the United States: Including a Study of the Rôle of Mixed-Blood Races Throughout the World* (Boston: R.G. Badger, 1918), 378.

7   Gary B. Nash, *Red, White, and Black: The Peoples of Early America* (Englewood Cliffs, NJ: Prentice-Hall, 1974), 287.

8   J.C Furnas, *Goodbye to Uncle Tom* (New York: W. Sloane Associates, 1956), 142.

9   Ibid., 149.

10   Ibid., 142.

11   Nash, *Red, White, and Black*, 289–90.

12   Charles Carroll, *The Negro a Beast; or, In the Image of God* (St. Louis: American Book and Bible House, 1900).

13   George M. Fredrickson, *The Black Image in the White Mind: The Debate on Afro-American Character and Destiny, 1817–1914* (New York: Harper & Row, 1971), 277.

14   Ibid.

15   Nella Larsen, *Passing* (New York: Penguin Books, 2003); James Whale, *Show Boat* (Universal Pictures, 1936).

16   William Lindsay White, *Lost Boundaries* (New York: Harcourt, Brace, 1948); Alfred L. Werker, *Lost Boundaries* (RD-DR Productions, 1949).

17   Delmer Daves, *Kings Go Forth* (United Artists, 1958).

18   Donald Bogle, *Toms, Coons, Mulattoes, Mammies, and Bucks: An Interpretive History of Blacks in American Films* (New York: Continuum, 1994), 192.

19   Elia Kazan, *Pinky* (Twentieth Century Fox, 1949).

20   Oscar Micheaux, *Within Our Gates* (Micheaux Book & Film Company, 1920); Oscar Micheaux, *God's Step Children*, (Micheaux Pictures Corporation, 1938).

21   Otto Preminger, *Carmen Jones* (Twentieth Century Fox, 1954); Robert Rossen, *Island in the Sun* (Twentieth Century Fox, 1957).

22   Elizabeth Ross Hayes was a social worker, sociologist, and a pioneer in the YWCA movement.

23   Mary Church Terrell was a feminist, civil rights activist, and the first president of the National Association of Colored Women.

24   "The Rise of Intermarriage," Pew Social & Demographic Trends, accessed March 17, 2013, http://www.pewsocialtrends.org/2012/02/16/the-rise-of-intermarriage/.

25   The most infamous Jezebel was a Phoenician princess who married Ahab, king of Israel, in the ninth century B.C. As queen she introduced the worship of Baal and sought to suppress the worship of Yahweh (Jehovah), the Hebrew God. She persecuted the prophets of Jehovah, many of whom she ordered to be killed. Her disregard for Jewish custom and her ruthless use of royal power are illustrated in the story involving Naboth, a Jezreelite. Jezebel falsely accused Naboth of treason. He was stoned to death. Then she and Ahab took possession of Naboth's vineyard. Her reign as queen was marked by similarly deceitful actions. The name Jezebel came to signify a deceitful and immoral woman. Her story is told in First Kings 18 and 19, and in Second Kings 9. In the New Testament book Revelations (2:20) the name Jezebel is used as a byword for apostasy.

26   K. Sue Jewell, *From Mammy to Miss America and Beyond: Cultural Images and the Shaping of US Social Policy* (London; New York: Routledge, 1993), 46.

27   Ibid., 46. Jewell uses "bad-black-girls" as a synonym for Black Jezebels.

28   See Deborah Gray White, *Ar'n't I a Woman?: Female Slaves in the Plantation South* (New York: W.W. Norton, 1999), 27–61. White's book is an excellent historical examination of the Jezebel portrayal, especially chapter one, "Jezebel and Mammy."

29   Ibid., 29.

30   In British North America, what we call racism did not really flower until the eighteenth century. In the seventeenth century, attitudes toward blacks and other non-whites tended to be more run-of-the-mill xenophobia. In the eighteenth century, this exploitation received ideological and "scientific" basis.

31   James Redpath and John R. McKivigan, *The Roving Editor; or, Talks with Slaves in the Southern States* (University Park: Pennsylvania State University Press, 1996), 141.

32   Frederick Douglass, *My Bondage and My Freedom* (New York: Arno Press, 1968), 60.

33   Henry Bibb and Lucius C. Matlack, *Narrative of the Life and Adventures of Henry Bibb, an American Slave* (New York: The author, 1849), 98–99, 112–16.

34   John D'Emilio and Estelle B. Freedman, *Intimate Matters: A History of Sexuality in America* (New York: Harper & Row, 1988), 102.

35   Ibid., 101.

36 Winthrop D. Jordan, *White over Black: American Attitudes towards the Negro, 1550–1812* (Baltimore: Penguin Books, 1969), 157 and note 44.

37 I considered using the word *pornographic* to describe the stripping and touching of slaves; however, pornography is more often associated with representations of people, and not the people themselves.

38 *The American Slave Vol. 12: Georgia Narratives; 1/2.* (Westport, CT: Greenwood Publ. Co., 1972), 228; Herbert G. Gutman, *The Black Family in Slavery and Freedom, 1750–1925* (New York: Pantheon Books, 1976), 77.

39 White, *Ar'n't I a Woman?*, 31.

40 D'Emilio and Freedman, *Intimate Matters*, 98.

41 Ibid., 104.

42 White, *Ar'n't I a Woman?*, 188, 189.

43 There is no date or manufacturer listed on the item or the cardboard box.

44 There is no date or manufacturer on the banner. Interestingly, there is a cloth flap covering her genital area; however, when lifted there is nothing there.

45 This postcard was produced by E.C. Kropp Company of Milwaukee, Wisconsin. It is a popular postcard as evidenced by its history of reproduction, which began in the 1950s and continued into the twenty-first century.

46 D.W. Griffith, *The Birth of a Nation* (David W. Griffith Corp., 1915).

47 Daniel J. Leab, *From Sambo to Superspade: The Black Experience in Motion Pictures* (Boston: Houghton Mifflin Co., 1976), 259.

48 Melvin Van Peebles, *Sweet Sweetback's Baadasssss Song* (Cinemation Industries, 1973).

49 Bogle, *Toms, Coons, Mulattoes, Mammies, and Bucks*, 236.

50 Arthur Knight, "Sex Stars," *Playboy's Sex in Cinema 4* (Chicago: Playboy Press, 1974), 142.

51 Bogle, *Toms, Coons, Mulattoes, Mammies, and Bucks*, 251.

52 Jack Hill, *Coffy* (American International Pictures, 1973); Jack Hill, *Foxy Brown* (American International Pictures, 1974); Jack Hill, *The Big Bird Cage* (New World Pictures, 1972); Arthur Roberson, *Street Sisters* (Movie Company, 1974); Frank Perry, *Dummy* (Warner Bros. Television, 1979); Alan Parker, *Angel Heart* (TriStar Pictures, 1987); Eddie Murphy, *Harlem Nights* (Paramount Pictures, 1989).

53 Martin Scorsese, *Taxi Driver* (Columbia Pictures, 1976); Woody Allen, *Deconstructing Harry* (Fine Line Features, 1997); Darrell Roodt, *Dangerous Ground* (New Line Cinema, 1997); Neil Jordan, *Mona Lisa* (Handmade Films, 1986).

54 Marc Forster, *Monster's Ball* (Lions Gate Films, 2002).

55 Allison Samuels, "Angela's Fire," *Newsweek* (July 1, 2002): 55.

56 Victor Fleming, *Gone with the Wind* (Selznick International Pictures, 1940); Ralph Nelson, *Lilies of the Field* (Rainbow Productions, 1963); Antoine Fuqua, *Training Day* (Warner Bros. Pictures, 2001).

57 In Marilyn Yarbrough and Crystal Bennett, "Cassandra and the 'Sistahs': The Peculiar Treatment of African American Women in the Myth of Women as Liars," *Journal of Gender, Race and Justice* (Spring 2000): 626–57, the authors use the words "evil, bitchy, stubborn and hateful" to describe the Sapphire.

58 John Ford, *Judge Priest* (Fox Film Corporation, 1934); George Marshall, *Music Is Magic* (Fox Film Corporation, 1935); David Butler, *The Little Colonel* (Fox Film Corporation, 1935); George Stevens, *Alice Adams* (RKO Radio Pictures, 1935); Jack Conway, *Saratoga* (Metro-Goldwyn-Mayer, 1937); Leigh Jason, *The Mad Miss Manton* (RKO Radio Pictures, 1938); Fleming, *Gone with the Wind*.

59 See, for example, *Amos 'n' Andy - I'se Regusted*, 2011, http://www.youtube.com/watch?v=BOIJqGeFnyI&feature=youtube_gdata_player (episode starts at approximately the 2:00 minute mark).

60 The peak of the show's popularity was 1930–31, when it attracted an audience of thirty to forty million people a night, six nights a week.

61 See, for example, *Amos 'n' Andy - Kingfish Sells A Lot*, 2012, http://www.youtube.com/watch?v=NQOtTHmwgm8&feature=youtube_gdata_player.

62 Jewell, *From Mammy to Miss America and Beyond*, 45.

63 "Bad Times on the Good Times Set," *Ebony* (September 1975).

64 Hill, *Coffy*.

65 "Transcript: 'FOX News Watch,' June 14, 2008," Fox News, December 7, 2011, http://www.foxnews.com/story/0,2933,367601,00.html.

66 Tim Story, *Barbershop* (Metro-Goldwyn-Mayer, 2002); Kevin Rodney Sullivan, *Barbershop 2: Back in Business* (Metro-Goldwyn-Mayer, 2004); Tyler Perry, *Why Did I Get Married?* (Lionsgate, 2007); "Angry African American Woman in a Purple Dress and Heels, Standing with Her Arms Crossed and Tapping Her Foot with a Stern Expression on Her Face Clipart Illustration Graphic by Dennis Cox #16467," accessed March 17, 2013, http://www.clipartof.com/portfolio/djart/illustration/angry-african-american-woman-in-a-purple-dress-and-heels-standing-with-her-arms-crossed-and-tapping-her-foot-with-a-stern-expression-on-her-face-16467.html; "African American Woman Looking Angry Stock Photos / Pictures / Photography / Royalty Free Images at Inmagine," accessed March 17, 2013, http://www.inmagine.com/bld108/bld108498-photo; Denene Millner, Angela Burt-Murray, and Mitzi Miller, *The Angry Black Woman's Guide to Life* (New York: Plume, 2004), accessed March 17, 2013, http://angryblackbitch.blogspot.com/.

67 Vanessa E. Jones, "The Angry Black Woman," Boston.com, April 20, 2004, http://www.boston.com/news/globe/living/articles/2004/04/20/the_angry_black_woman/.

68 Lorien Olive, "Omarosa Obama: Sapphire Lives," *Roadkill Politics: A White Working Class Perspective on Politics*, April 15, 2008, roadkillpolitics.blogspot.com.

CHAPTER SIX

1 Donald Bogle, *Toms, Coons, Mulattoes, Mammies, and Bucks: An Interpretive History of Blacks in American Films* (New York: Continuum, 1994), 8.

2 For an excellent discussion of the work environment of slaves read Kenneth M. Stampp, *The Peculiar Institution: Slavery in the Ante-bellum South* (New York: Knopf, 1956), chapter 3.

3 Ibid., 79–80.

4 Ibid., 85.

5 Ibid., 81.

6 Ibid., 63.

7 Thomas Nelson Page, *The Negro: The Southerner's Problem* (New York: C. Scribner's Sons, 1904), 80.

8 David Katz and Kenneth Braley, "Racial Stereotypes of One Hundred College Students," *Journal of Abnormal and Social Psychology* 28 (1933): 280–90.

9 G.M. Gilbert, "Stereotype Persistence and Change among College Students," *Journal of Abnormal and Social Psychology* 46 (1951): 245–54.

10 L. Duke, "But Some of My Best Friends Are . . . ," *Washington Post*, January 14, 1991.

11 Martin Gilens, *Why Americans Hate Welfare: Race, Media, and the Politics of Antipoverty Policy* (Chicago: University of Chicago Press, 1999).

12 *The Wooing and Wedding of a Coon* (Selig Polyscope Company, 1907); T. Wharton, *How Rastus Got His Turkey* (Pathé Frères, 1910); *Coontown Suffragettes* (General Film Company, 1914).

13 Paul Sloane, *Hearts in Dixie* (Fox Film Corporation, 1929).

14 Daniel J. Leab, *From Sambo to Superspade: The Black Experience in Motion Pictures* (Boston: Houghton Mifflin Co., 1976), 86.

15 George Marshall, *In Old Kentucky* (Fox Film Corporation, 1935).

16 Leab, *From Sambo to Superspade*, 89.

17 Hamilton MacFadden, *Stand Up and Cheer!* (Fox Film Corporation, 1934).

18 Bogle, *Toms, Coons, Mulattoes, Mammies, and Bucks*, 41.

19 *Black History: Lost, Stolen, or Strayed* (Columbia Broadcasting System, 1968).

20   Bogle, *Toms, Coons, Mulattoes, Mammies, and Bucks*, 44.

21   James Cruze, *David Harum* (Fox Film Corporation, 1934); John Ford, *Judge Priest* (Fox Film Corporation, 1934).

22   James H. Dormon, "Shaping the Popular Image of Post-Reconstruction American Blacks: The 'Coon Song' Phenomenon of the Gilded Age," *American Quarterly* 40 (December 1988): 453–65.

23   Robert C. Toll, *On with the Show!: The First Century of Show Business in America* (New York: Oxford University Press, 1976), 118.

24   Charles H. Smith, "Have American Negroes Too Much Liberty?," *Forum* 16 (1893): 181.

25   C.R. Breckinridge, "Speech of the Honorable Clifton R. Breckinridge," in *Race Problems of the South: Report of the Proceedings of the First Annual Conference Held Under the Auspices of the Southern Society for the Promotion of the Study of Race Conditions and Problems in the South, at Montgomery, Alabama, May 8, 9, 10, A.D. 1900,* by Southern Society for the Promotion of the Study of Race Conditions and Problems in the South (Richmond, VA: B.F. Johnson Pub. Co., 1900), 174.

26   George T. Winston, "The Relations of the Whites to the Negroes," *Annals of the American Academy of Political and Social Science* 17 (1901): 108–9.

27   Thomas Nelson Page, *Red Rock: A Chronicle of Reconstruction* (New York: Charles Scribner's Sons, 1898), 356–58.

28   Barbara Holden-Smith, "Lynching, Federalism, and the Intersection of Race and Gender in the Progressive Era," *Yale Journal of Law and Feminism* 31 (1996): 1, http://library2.lawschool.cornell.edu/hein/Holden-Smith,%20Barbara%208%20Yale%20J.L.%20&%20Feminism%2031%201996.pdf.

29   George M. Fredrickson, *The Black Image in the White Mind; The Debate on Afro-American Character and Destiny, 1817–1914* (New York: Harper & Row, 1971), 279.

30   Thomas Dixon, *The Leopard's Spots: A Romance of the White Man's Burden—1865–1900,* (New York: Grosset & Dunlap, 1902); Fredrickson, *The Black Image in the White Mind*, 280.

31   Thomas Dixon, *The Clansman: An Historical Romance of the Ku Klux Klan* (New York, N.Y.: Grosset & Dunlap, 1905); Fredrickson, *The Black Image in the White Mind*, 280–81.

32   D.W. Griffith, *The Birth of a Nation* (David W. Griffith Corp., 1915).

33   Gibson, "The Negro Holocaust: Lynching and Race Riots in the United States, 1880–1950," 5.

34   Holden-Smith, "Lynching, Federalism, and the Intersection of Race and Gender in the Progressive Era," 14.

35   Ibid., 15.

36   Ibid., 16.

37   Ibid., 14.

38   Ibid., 16.

39   Ibid.

40   Gibson, "The Negro Holocaust: Lynching and Race Riots in the United States, 1880–1950," 3.

41   Allen Day Grimshaw, *Racial Violence in the United States* (Chicago: Aldine Pub. Co., 1969), 264–65.

42   Griffith, *The Birth of a Nation.*

43   Paul Schrader, *American Gigolo* (Paramount Pictures, 1980); Steven Spielberg, *The Color Purple* (Warner Bros. Pictures, 1985); Brian Gibson, *What's Love Got to Do with It* (Buena Vista Pictures, 1993).

44   Antoine Fuqua, *Training Day* (Warner Bros. Pictures, 2001).

45   Charles Ogletree, "The Basic Black Forum with Charles Ogletree," n.d.

46   Chase Squires and Ralph Greer Jr., "Frustration Mounts in Search," The Hoax Project, October 30, 1994, http://jclass.umd.edu/archive/newshoax/casestudies/crime/CrimeSmith1030a.html.

47   Reginald Fields, "Black Residents Hurt, Angered," The Hoax Project, November 4, 1994, http://jclass.umd.edu/archive/newshoax/casestudies/crime/CrimeSmith1104c.html.

CHAPTER SEVEN

1   Jeremy W. Peters, "Auctioning Memories in a Town Haunted by the Klan," *New York Times*, May 23, 2005, http://www.nytimes.com/2005/05/23/national/23klan.html.
2   Greg Kaza, "Hitler's Klanarchist," *Fifth Estate* 326, vol. 22, no. 2 (Summer 1987): 16.
3   The objects came from at least ten different sources—all paying 20 percent commission to the auctioneer.
4   For more information about the role of women in Klan organizations, read Kathleen M. Blee, *Women of the Klan: Racism and Gender in the 1920s* (Berkeley: University of California Press, 1991).
5   See, for example, "Bidding on KKK Items Raises Stir in Mich.," MSNBC.com, accessed March 13, 2013, http://www.nbcnews.com/id/6884978/ns/us_news-life/t/bidding-kkk-items-raises-stir-mich/.

Index

Page numbers in *italic* refer to illustrations. "Passim" (literally "scattered") indicates intermittent discussion of a topic over a cluster of pages.

ABOUT PM PRESS

PM Press was founded at the end of 2007 by a small collection of folks with decades of publishing, media, and organizing experience. PM Press co-conspirators have published and distributed hundreds of books, pamphlets, CDs, and DVDs. Members of PM have founded enduring book fairs, spearheaded victorious tenant organizing campaigns, and worked closely with bookstores, academic conferences, and even rock bands to deliver political and challenging ideas to all walks of life. We're old enough to know what we're doing and young enough to know what's at stake.

We seek to create radical and stimulating fiction and non-fiction books, pamphlets, T-shirts, visual and audio materials to entertain, educate, and inspire you. We aim to distribute these through every available channel with every available technology—whether that means you are seeing anarchist classics at our bookfair stalls, reading our latest vegan cookbook at the café, downloading geeky fiction e-books, or digging new music and timely videos from our website.

PM Press is always on the lookout for talented and skilled volunteers, artists, activists, and writers to work with. If you have a great idea for a project or can contribute in some way, please get in touch.

PM Press
PO Box 23912
Oakland, CA 94623
www.pmpress.org

ABOUT BETWEEN THE LINES

Founded in 1977, Between the Lines publishes books that support social change and justice. Our goal is not private gain, nor are we owned by a faceless conglomerate. We are cooperatively run by our employees and a small band of volunteers who share a tenacious belief in books, authors, and ideas that break new ground.

Between the Lines books present new ideas and challenge readers to rethink the world around them. Our authors offer analysis of historical events and contemporary issues not often found in the mainstream. We specialize in informative, non-fiction books on politics and public policy, social issues, history, international development, gender and sexuality, critical race issues, culture, adult and popular education, labour and work, environment, technology, and media.

"Who is your leader?"
We create high-quality books that promote equitable social change, and we reflect our mission in the way our organization is structured. BTL has no bosses, no owners. It's the product of what some would likely describe as "sixties idealism"—what we call political principles. Our small office staff and Editorial Committee make decisions—from what to publish to how to run the place—by consensus. Our Editorial Committee includes a number of original and long-time members, as well as several younger academics and community activists eager to carry on the publishing work started by the generation before them.

www.btlbooks.com

FRIENDS OF PM PRESS

These are indisputably momentous times—the financial system is melting down globally and the Empire is stumbling. Now more than ever there is a vital need for radical ideas.

In the years since its founding—and on a mere shoestring—PM Press has risen to the formidable challenge of publishing and distributing knowledge and entertainment for the struggles ahead. With over 300 releases to date, we have published an impressive and stimulating array of literature, art, music, politics, and culture. Using every available medium, we've succeeded in connecting those hungry for ideas and information to those putting them into practice.

Friends of PM allows you to directly help impact, amplify, and revitalize the discourse and actions of radical writers, filmmakers, and artists. It provides us with a stable foundation from which we can build upon our early successes and provides a much-needed subsidy for the materials that can't necessarily pay their own way. You can help make that happen—and receive every new title automatically delivered to your door once a month—by joining as a Friend of PM Press. And, we'll throw in a free T-shirt when you sign up.

Here are your options:

- **$30 a month** Get all books and pamphlets plus 50% discount on all webstore purchases

- **$40 a month** Get all PM Press releases (including CDs and DVDs) plus 50% discount on all webstore purchases

- **$100 a month** Superstar—Everything plus PM merchandise, free downloads, and 50% discount on all webstore purchases

For those who can't afford $30 or more a month, we're introducing **Sustainer Rates** at $15, $10 and $5. Sustainers get a free PM Press T-shirt and a 50% discount on all purchases from our website.

Your Visa or Mastercard will be billed once a month, until you tell us to stop. Or until our efforts succeed in bringing the revolution around. Or the financial meltdown of Capital makes plastic redundant. Whichever comes first.

Speaking OUT: Queer Youth in Focus

Rachelle Lee Smith, with a foreword by Candace Gingrich
and an afterword by Graeme Taylor

ISBN: 978-1-62963-041-0
$14.95   128 pages

Speaking OUT: Queer Youth in Focus is a photographic essay that explores a wide spectrum of experiences told from the perspective of a diverse group of young people, ages fourteen to twenty-four, identifying as queer (i.e., lesbian, gay, bisexual, transgender, or questioning). Portraits are presented without judgment or stereotype by eliminating environmental influence with a stark white backdrop. This backdrop acts as a blank canvas, where each subject's personal thoughts are handwritten onto the final photographic print. With more than sixty-five portraits photographed over a period of ten years, *Speaking OUT* provides rare insight into the passions, confusions, prejudices, joys, and sorrows felt by queer youth.

Speaking OUT gives a voice to an underserved group of people that are seldom heard and often silenced. The collaboration of image and first-person narrative serves to provide an outlet, show support, create dialogue, and help those who struggle. It not only shows unity within the LGBTQ community, but also commonalities regardless of age, race, gender, and sexual orientation.

With recent media attention and the success of initiatives such as the It Gets Better Project, resources for queer youth have grown. Still, a void exists which *Speaking OUT* directly addresses: this book is for youth, by youth.

Speaking OUT is an award-winning, nationally and internationally shown and published body of work. These images have been published in magazines such as the *Advocate*, *School Library Journal*, *Curve*, *Girlfriends*, and *Out*, and showcased by the Human Rights Campaign, National Public Radio, Public Television, and the U.S. Department of Education. The work continues to show in galleries, universities, youth centers, and churches around the world.

"Rachelle Lee Smith has created a book that is not only visually stunning but also gripping with powerful words and even more inspiring young people! This is an important work of art! I highly recommend buying it and sharing it!"
—Perez Hilton, blogger and television personality

"It's often said that our youth are our future. In the LGBT community, before they become the future we must help them survive today. This book showcases the diversity of creative imagination it takes to get us to tomorrow."
—Mark Segal, award-winning LGBT journalist

"The power of a look, a pose, and a story can be seen through Rachelle Lee Smith's photography and the youth who opened up their raw emotions, insecurities, and celebrations to us all. Sharing stories saves lives, but also reminds us that there can be continual struggle in finding identity and acceptance."
—Ryan Sallans, author of *Second Son: Transitioning Toward My Destiny, Love and Life*

Basic Skills Caucasian Americans Workbook

Beverly Hope Slapin with Guillermo Prado

ISBN: 978-1-60486-520-2
$14.95   128 pages

The world of the Caucasian Americans comes alive through satirical history lessons, puzzles, and word games for all ages. The history, material culture, mores, and lifeways of the people now collectively known as the "Caucasian Americans" have often been discussed but rarely comprehended. Until now. This revised edition of *Basic Skills Caucasian Americans Workbook* provides young readers with accurate accounts of the lives of the Caucasian Americans, who long ago roamed our land. Caucasians are as much a part of American life as they were one hundred years ago. Even in times past, Caucasians were not all the same. Not all of them lived in gated communities or drove SUVs. They were not all techie geeks or power-hungry bankers. Some were hostile, but many were friendly.

It is important for young people to study our Caucasian American forebears in order to learn how they enriched the heritage and history of the world. We hope that the youngsters who read these pages will realize the role that Caucasian Americans played in shaping the United States, and in making the world the remarkable place that it is today.

"For many years, I've recommended this amazing book as anthropological source material in the education of young children. Beverly Slapin has captured the essence of what it was really like to have lived as a Caucasian American."
—Virginia Lea, Ph.D., Associate Professor of Education, University of Wisconsin-Stout, Menominee, Wisconsin; Co-Chair, Proposals Committee, National Association for Multicultural Education; Executive Director, Educultural Foundation; Co-Chair, Pride Alliance, University of Wisconsin-Stout, Menominee, Wisconsin

"Every public library that values a balanced social studies section must have this 'go-to' resource on understanding Caucasian Americans. Delightful illustrations, word scrambles and other exercises make it fun as well as truly educational; and it makes a great recommendation for family car trips."
—Nina Lindsay, Children's Services Librarian, Oakland Public Library, Oakland, California; Caucasian American member of the American Library Association

"This remarkable work is key to understanding the abstruse and non-intuitive premises underlying the Caucasian worldview and motivational impeti."
—Annie Esposito, Local News Director Emerita, KPFA-FM, Berkeley, California; Copublisher Emerita, *Mendocino Country Independent*

World War 3 Illustrated: 1979-2014

Edited by Peter Kuper and Seth Tobocman
with an introduction by Bill Ayers

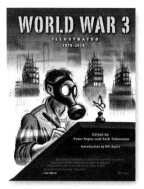

ISBN: 978-1-60486-958-3
$29.95   320 pages

Founded in 1979 by Seth Tobocman and Peter Kuper, *World War 3 Illustrated* is a labor of love run by a collective of artists (both first-timers and established professionals) and political activists working with the unified goal of creating a home for political comics, graphics, and stirring personal stories. Their confrontational comics shine a little reality on the fantasy world of the American kleptocracy, and have inspired the developing popularity and recognition of comics as a respected art form.

This full-color retrospective exhibition is arranged thematically, including housing rights, feminism, environmental issues, religion, police brutality, globalization, and depictions of conflicts from the Middle East to the Midwest. *World War 3 Illustrated* isn't about a war that may happen; it's about the ongoing wars being waged around the world and on our very own doorsteps. *World War 3 Illustrated* also illuminates the war we wage on each other—and sometimes the one taking place in our own minds. *World War 3* artists have been covering the topics that matter for over 30 years, and they're just getting warmed up.

Contributors include Sue Coe, Eric Drooker, Fly, Sandy Jimenez, Sabrina Jones, Peter Kuper, Mac McGill, Kevin Pyle, Spain Rodriguez, Nicole Schulman, Seth Tobocman, Susan Willmarth, and dozens more.

"World War 3 Illustrated *is the real thing. . . . As always it mixes newcomers and veterans, emphasizes content over style (but has plenty of style), keeps that content accessible and critical, and pays its printers and distributors but no one else. If it had nothing more than that kind of dedication to recommend it, it would be invaluable. But it has much, much more.*"
—*New York Times*

"*Reading* WW3 *is both a cleansing and an enraging experience. The graphics remind us how very serious the problems and how vile the institutions that cause them really are.*"
—*Utne Reader*

"*Powerful graphic art and comic strips from the engaged and enraged pens of urban artists. The subjects include poverty, war, homelessness and drugs; it's a poke in the eye from the dark side of America, tempered by what the artists describe as their 'oppositional optimism.'*"
—*Whole Earth Review*

"*This is art—not marketing—on the newsstand. It represents the sort of creativity too rarely given an outlet in comics. It's the best and longest running alternative comics anthology around.*"
—*Comics Journal*

This Is Not a Photo Opportunity: The Street Art of Banksy

Banksy with photographs by Martin Bull

ISBN: 978-1-62963-036-6
$20.00   176 pages

This Is Not a Photo Opportunity is a street-level, full-color showcase of some of Banksy's most innovative pieces ever.

Banksy, Britain's now-legendary "guerilla" street artist, has painted the walls, streets, and bridges of towns and cities throughout the world. Once viewed as vandalism, Banksy's work is now venerated, collected, and preserved.

Over the course of a decade, Martin Bull has documented dozens of the most important and impressive works by the legendary political artist, most of which are no longer in existence. *This Is Not a Photo Opportunity* boasts nearly 200 color photos of Banksy's public work on the walls, as seen from the streets.

"We are concerned that Banksy's street art glorifies what is essentially vandalism."
—Diane Shakespeare, Keep Britain Tidy

"It may be art, but it should not be permitted."
—Michael Bloomberg, former mayor of New York City

"One original thought is worth 1000 meaningless quotes."
—Banksy